# ALBUQUERQUE TRIVIA

By
Cynthia and Arthur Romero

ISBN 0-7414-3761-9

*Published by:*

INFINITY
PUBLISHING.COM

*1094 New DeHaven Street, Suite 100*
*West Conshohocken, PA 19428-2713*
*Info@buybooksontheweb.com*
*www.buybooksontheweb.com*
*Toll-free (877) BUY BOOK*
*Local Phone (610) 941-9999*
*Fax (610) 941-9959*

*Printed in the United States of America*

*Printed on Recycled Paper*

*Published May 2007*

# Disclaimer

The purpose of this book is for the entertainment of the reader. The authors have used their best efforts to present facts and figures about Albuquerque. The authors have no claim as to absolute authenticity of any time, place or events stated herein.

# About the Cover Photo

The "building glow" for this Albuquerque skyline image was orchestrated by John Yost and Marble Street Studio, Inc. Starting in mid-November of 1999, they contacted 24 building managers and asked their help in creating the photo shoot. All promised their help and agreed to leave their lights on until 6:00 p.m. on December 17$^{th}$. The sunset that day was at 4:57 p.m. According to the photographer, the city was cold, calm and clearly beautiful. The photo was taken from atop the Channel 13 studios near Coal Avenue and 14$^{th}$ Street. John Yost says that his studio can hardly claim sole credit for the image. The cooperation that he received from all the building managers and their clients proved to be truly representative of the entire city. The special "glow" represents to us the heart of Albuquerque.

# Foreword

By
Marc Simmons,
Historian

In 2006, Albuquerque commemorated the 300th anniversary of its founding. Among America's cities west of the Mississippi, only neighboring Santa Fe is older. During the long and sometimes turbulent three centuries of its existence, Albuquerque has accumulated a history so rich and varied that, as far as human interest goes, it can rival most other municipalities.

The city's story actually began with the Spanish explorer Francisco Vásquez de Coronado who first spent the winter of 1540-1541 in the Albuquerque valley. Other expeditions followed, including in 1598 the one led by Don Juan de Oñate, the man charged with carving out Spain's frontier province of New Mexico.

During the 1600s, several Spanish estancias, or ranches, flourished inside the wide boundaries of today's Albuquerque. But they were swept away, with all else that was European, in the great Pueblo revolt of 1680.

In the wake of the Spanish reconquest of the 1690s, the royal government launched a vigorous effort to restore what had been lost, and in the process the humble Villa de Albuquerque was born in 1706. The town struggled and grew during the remainder of the colonial period, saw the beginning of change after independence in 1821, and following the American conquest of the Mexican territory in 1846, it started to reshape itself and adopt a new identity.

With the 1880 arrival of the railroad, Albuquerque's march toward modernity began in earnest. The process continues to this day, with the prospect of a one million population looming on the not too distant horizon. The city's 2006 birthday provides all of Albuquerque an opportunity to reflect on the past and to chart new directions for the future.

Unlike most quiz books on trivia, this one by Cynthia and Arthur Romero, Albuquerque Trivia, is highly focused, offering at the same time answers that are substantive and to the point. Further, the fine collection of historical illustrations that is included, drawn mainly from the photo archives of the Albuquerque Museum, imparts a visual sense of what the city was like in days gone by.

And finally, Albuquerque Trivia is just plain fun to read, having entertainment value, as well as being educational. I've enjoyed it immensely and am pleased that my friends the Romeros have seen fit to bring out this second, updated edition. Like the previous edition, this handy little volume is so well put together that I have no hesitation in recommending it to anyone needing a quick, introductory view of Albuquerque, yesterday and today. You won't be disappointed!

# Introduction

Happy Birthday, Albuquerque! In 2006, Albuquerque celebrated its 300th year as a city.

The events that shape Albuquerque's history make it a unique, charming, and diverse city. Our collection of trivia brings together facts regarding our city's people, places, and occurrences over three hundred years. Albuquerque's climate and scenery alone are factors that have drawn people to our city over the years, making it a city that is hard to forget. This publication includes prestigious national rankings that include Albuquerque in top ten lists, which may contribute to finally putting Albuquerque on the map of the USA.

This book is for long time residents, newcomers and visitors to this wonderful city who want to learn factual history and information in a fun and entertaining context that is an easy to read guide.

We would like to thank the Albuquerque Museum for the use of their wonderful historical photographs and for their involvement and time spent on our project. A special thanks goes to Glenn in the Photo Archives Department.

We are honored to have Marc Simmons, famed New Mexico historian and author of several books on Albuquerque and New Mexico, review our book for both of its publications.

We are proud to live and work here; we love Albuquerque!

Cynthia and Arthur Romero

# Table of Contents

# The Diversity of Albuquerque

**How often is Albuquerque mistaken for a foreign city or for a U.S. city that is more primitive than modern?**

According to the Albuquerque Convention and Visitors Bureau, they receive one call a month. These are calls from people asking if they can drink the water here, if they need a passport, or if it is possible to get a hotel room with air conditioning. There are even inquiries about whether currency exchange is necessary. In 1993, there was an average of five inquiries a week of this nature.

In Richard C. Sandoval's book, *One of Our Fifty is Missing (A Continuing Saga)*, he shares several incidents in which the state of New Mexico is mistaken for a foreign country. He recounts several incidents by Albuquerqueans in which they have received mail from out of state that has been through customs. Or they have sent mail out of state and the receiver is asked to pay customs before obtaining it. Maybe residents should add 'U.S.A.' to Albuquerque, New Mexico on correspondence in order to inform the U.S. Postal Service of our statehood.

**Where is Albuquerque located in the U.S.A.?**

Albuquerque is equidistant from Los Angeles and Kansas City, from New Orleans and San Francisco, from Phoenix and Denver, and from Salt Lake City and Dallas.

**What Albuquerque hotel was built in 1939 by Conrad Hilton?**

The Albuquerque Hilton, now known as La Posada de Albuquerque, which captures the spirit and charm of New Mexico. It is located at 125 2nd St. NW. The hotel boasted modern amenities for its time, including air conditioning, an elevator, and roof top solariums that offered massage services.

Conrad Hilton and Zsa Zsa Gabor entertained friends at their engagement dinner at the Albuquerque Hilton. The hotel was a political stop for many national candidates and John F. Kennedy delivered a tribute at the hotel to the late New Mexico Governor, Edmund G. Ross. A meeting was held at the hotel in 1945 that was the basis for the government's espionage case against Ethel and Julius Rosenberg. A registration card from the hotel was the one piece of evidence that established the meeting.

The Hilton chain sold the hotel in the early 1970s. In 1983, Southwest Resorts became the hotel's owner and obtained the designation of the hotel on the National Register of Historic Places. The Goodman Realty Group rescued the hotel from bankruptcy in 2005, and plans a major renovation.

**Which event is the best race in New Mexico according to Runner's World Magazine?**

The annual Run for the Zoo. Proceeds benefit the Rio Grande Zoo. The Run for the Zoo consists of the 10K, 5K and 1 mile races. It is quite possibly the largest high-altitude running event in the U.S.

La Posada Hotel (Hilton), Second St., 1950s. Photographer Harvey Caplin. The Albuquerque Museum Photoarchives, PA1982.180.606.

**Why have world-class runners been coming to Albuquerque to train for the past forty years?**

Albuquerque does have mild temperatures and hilly terrain, but it is the training at this high altitude that makes a runner's performance at sea level better.

Former UNM track and field coach Hugh Hackett began recruiting foreign athletes in the 1960s.

In 2004, Romania's Gabriela Szabo, who won the 2000 Olympic women's gold medal in the 5,000 meters, trained in Albuquerque, at the Eldorado High School track.[1]

**What city used to be a suburb of Albuquerque and lured Easterners by its description of being a retirement community?**

Rio Rancho, New Mexico, incorporated as a city on September 3, 1980. Its parents are known as American Realty and Petroleum Company.

Despite being marketed as a retirement community, Rio Rancho's population is the youngest in the state. It is also the state's fastest growing city, as well as one of the fastest growing in the country. Known as "Little New York" years ago, its estimated population is now over 62,000. Before the first homes were built in 1962, it was empty desert. Rio Rancho is situated at the northwestern end of Albuquerque.

Old Town, Gribera Restaurant, 1892. (The restaurant sign advertises, “MEALS AT ALL HOURS 15 & 25¢” and “ROOMS FOR RENT 25 & 50¢.”) The Albuquerque Museum Photoarchives, PA1973.12.9.

**With the arrival of the railroad, what does author Erna Fergusson contend was the factor of all growth in Albuquerque?**

She says it was the "Gringo element" always pushing for the railroad, the "Restless Gringos" always wanting new things and new ways in which to run this backward city living in the "land of mañana." Growth occurred because of compromise by the "Gringos" who moved to Albuquerque advocating change and industrialization and the Spanish-American citizenry, who resisted it. It stands to reason that Albuquerque today would not be what it has become without either element.

**What was the reason for the city's continued growth in the 1940s?**

The city was an ideal spot for Federal programming. Millions of dollars went into the Sandia Corporation, the Atomic Energy Commission, Sandia Base, Manzano Base, Kirtland Air Force Base, along with the Indian School and the Indian Hospital, which was also maintained by the government.

**After the Jesuits assumed the operation of San Felipe de Neri Church, what was it that they began extensive cultivation in?**

The Jesuits began extensive cultivation of Mission grapes for wine after they assumed the operation of San Felipe de Neri Church in 1868. Albuquerque once produced large quantities of fine Southwestern wines.

**Where was the mercantile and entertainment district in the 1880s?**

Railroad Avenue was the mercantile and entertainment district with clothing stores, restaurants, hotels, theaters, general stores, and saloons in abundance.

**What did the Spaniards consider to be one of the Albuquerque Valley's finest natural resources?**

The cottonwood tree. The wood is lightweight, long-fibered, and soft but tough. It provided fence posts, corral poles, timbers for architectural purposes, and material for a variety of agricultural and domestic purposes, including carts, plow beams, and kitchen utensils. Cottonwood also makes good fuel. Still today, Pueblo Indians on the river like to burn it because it produces a hot fire and leaves little ash.[2]

**What is the elevation of Albuquerque and of Sandia Peak?**

Albuquerque is at an elevation of 5,314 feet. It actually ranges from 4,900 feet above sea level in the valley to 6,500 feet in the foothills of the Northeast Heights. North Sandia Peak (where visitors can drive to) rises to an elevation of 10,378 feet. Sandia Crest, at an altitude of 9,782 feet, can be reached by tram or can be hiked to from the base of the ski area or from the base of the western side of the Sandia Mountains via the La Luz trail.

**What invigorating and curative resource has lured thousands to Albuquerque?**

Sunlight, which is abundant here. There are only five days a year, on an average, in which the sky is completely overcast and the sun does not shine. During one record stretch (between December 1961 and February 1964) the sun shone, at least briefly, for 779 consecutive days. One hundred days a year, on the average, are virtually cloudless.

The benefits of sunlight for humans have been recognized for centuries. This was the curative resource that lured thousands of sufferers of tuberculosis and other pulmonary ailments to Albuquerque in the nineteenth and early twentieth centuries.[3]

**Why are tornadoes rare for Albuquerque?**

According to meteorologists, it is the Sandia mountains that keep the Albuquerque valley free from tornadoes. Their 10,000 plus foot height shields the city from the kinds of violent storms that periodically strike the plains of the central United States. There is an exception to every rule, however. A twister occurred here in the 1980s and did minor damage to an office building in the northeast section of town.

**How is Christmas celebrated in Albuquerque?**

¡Feliz Navidad y Prospero Año Nuevo (Merry Christmas and Happy New Year)! Christmas in Albuquerque is similar to Christmas around the state of New Mexico. For many, the holiday begins on December 12, Our Lady of Gudalupe's day, commemorating the legend of the

Old Town Plaza, 1980. Photographer Steve Donahue. The Albuquerque Museum Photoarchives, PA2000.25.35.

appearance of Nuestra Señora de Guadalupe (Our Lady of Guadalupe) to a poor Indian man named Juan Diego in Mexico in 1531. Then on December 16, the 9-day celebration of Las Posadas begins. (La Posada means "the inn.") Many New Mexicans reenact the Biblical story of Mary and Joseph searching for a place to spend the night. Again and again, admission is denied until finally, a place is found for the Santo Niño, the Christ child, to be born.

Christmas decorations include "farolitos" (little lanterns), also known as luminarias (candles, sand and paper bags). Their purpose is to light the way for the Christ child. It is traditional on Christmas Eve – la Noche Buena – to feast on posole, biscochitos, tamales and tortillas.

**In the face of sickness and the constant threat of Indian raid, how did Albuquerque's people find solace?**

In religion, which has always been the touchstone of Hispanic life.

**What is the population of the Albuquerque metro area?**

As of 2005, Albuquerque had 484,246 residents. The population of the metro area (which includes Bernalillo, Sandoval and Valencia counties) was 766,016.

**How much of the state's population is settled in Albuquerque?**

Just under one third.

Carving of the Virgin Mary in tree in Old Town.

**In what year was Albuquerque voted the cleanest city in the country?**

1988.

**What is one result of the city's mile-high altitude?**

The atmosphere is significantly thinner than at sea level, containing 17% less oxygen for a given volume.

**How many different plant species can be found in the vegetation of the Sandia Mountains?**

More than 890 different plant species.

**Why did the Northeast Heights area of Albuquerque expand so rapidly?**

Two reasons: The attraction of the defense-related industries which grew around Sandia Base and Kirtland Air Force Base and the availability of large tracts of land with clear titles.

**What are the names of Albuquerque's three major indoor shopping malls?**

Winrock Center (built by Winthrop Rockefeller on land owned by the University), which opened in 1961; Coronado Mall, which opened two years later, also in northeast Albuquerque; and Cottonwood Mall, which opened in 1996 and is located on the city's west side.

**Where is the business located that sports a twelve foot high chainsaw sculpture of a lumberjack?**

K & S Service Center at 7521 Menaul NE.

**How many miles does the city of Albuquerque encompass?**

133 square miles.

**How many inhabitants did the Albuquerque census show one hundred years after its founding?**

A population of 635.

**What was the highest temperature recorded for Albuquerque?**

107 degrees on June 26, 1994.[4]

The first 11 months of 2003 were the warmest in recorded history in New Mexico, according to federal climate scientists.[5]

**What was the lowest temperature recorded for Albuquerque?**

Seventeen degrees below zero on January 7, 1971.[6]

**Which park is the oldest in Albuquerque?**

Robinson Park, which is located downtown, near 10th and Central. The land for this park was donated by the Atlantic and Pacific, a division of the Santa Fe Railroad. It was named after the local district manager's daughter.[7]

**What is Albuquerque's distinction in recent national business rankings?**

In May, 2005, Albuquerque was featured on MSN Moncy, ranked by Forbes in their top five, as a Best City to Start a Business or Career. Forbes based their decision on the fact that Albuquerque was a metro area that stood out when it came to keeping costs down and attracting smart people.[8]

In May, 2006, Albuquerque was ranked number one by Forbes for the Best Places in the Nation for Business and Careers. Forbes' reasoning was that Albuquerque had the lowest business costs in the country, 24% below the national average. They also felt that Albuquerque benefited from an educated population and rising household income.

In May, 2006, Kiplinger's Personal Finance ranked Albuquerque 3rd Smartest City to Live out of 50. Some of the criteria used to pick were: reasonable cost of living (an attractive house for between $300,000-400,000), access to quality health care, and a strong economy.

Looking North on Santiago St. (Romero St.), 1885. The Albuquerque Museum Photoarchives, PA1978.50.99.

In January, 2006, Albuquerque was ranked by USA Today as one of their top six destinations in the world for 2006. The other five destinations for the year were China, Croatia, Thailand, The Netherlands, and Turkey. USA Today talked about Albuquerque hosting its tricentennial, its Museums of Art and History, and the upcoming International Balloon Fiesta.

Albuquerque was named 10th Fittest City in the Nation in January, 2005 and the 13th Fittest City in the Nation in January, 2006 by Men's Fitness Magazine. This magazine compiles a list of 25 Fittest Cities and 25 Fattest Cities.[9]

**What are Albuquerque's sister cities?**

Alburquerque, Spain

Ashgabat, Turkmenistan

Chihuahua, Mexico

Guadalajara, Mexico

Helmstedt, Germany

Hualien, Taiwan

Lanzhou, China

Sasebo, Japan

**How many of the earth's seven life zones does a ride on the Sandia Peak Tram pass through?**

Four. The 2.7 mile tram ride, in biological terms, is the equivalent of going from Mexico to Alaska in twenty minutes.

**What is the "Chevy on a Stick"?**

On the northwest corner of Gibson and San Mateo you will find, much to your amazement, a 1954 Chevrolet, covered with blue tile and mounted forty feet off the ground.

**Have there ever been UFO sightings in Albuquerque?**

Through June and July of 1947, the Albuquerque Journal gave almost daily front page accounts of the sightings. During this same summer, more UFO sightings were reported in New Mexico than in any other state.

On July 1, 1947, a blue saucer was reported over Albuquerque, zigzagging across the sky. On another occasion, a whole line of thirteen silver discs flew over the city. That summer, people frequently watched from their front lawns as the "space-ships" performed acrobatics above them.[10]

**Who are Albuquerque's two astronauts?**

Mike Mullane, a St. Pius High School graduate, and Sidney Gutierrez, a Valley High graduate. Mullane was part of the first group of NASA space shuttle astronauts in 1978. He retired in 1990. Gutierrez became a shuttle astronaut in 1984 and piloted the Columbia in 1991.[11]

Chevy on a stick.

**The Albuquerque – Santa Fe – Taos area is third in the country only to the East Coast and West Coast in the sales of what commodity?**

Art.[12]

**What constitutes the most popular foods eaten in Albuquerque?**

The same menus that are another reflection of the tricultural diversity of the whole state of New Mexico. Most New Mexican foods contain chile. Chile has a long, unique history. Chile grew as a wild perennial from South America north into Mexico. It was cultivated by prehistoric Indians, and was a main nutritional source for the Indians of Peru in 1000 B.C.

Nothing speaks of the uniqueness of New Mexican cooking more than green or red chile. Chilis are excellent in a sauce for casseroles, enchiladas, tamales, or to make salsa dips.

**How long has chile been popular in New Mexico?**

The roots of chile in New Mexico go back at least as far as 1598, when Don Juan de Oñate entered the state. The Pueblo Indians and early Spanish colonists claimed that chile was a good preservative, natural digestive, herbal medicine, and disinfectant for wounds. The chile in New Mexico is good, whether it comes from the north, in the foothills of the Sangre de Cristo Mountains, or from the lower area of the Hatch/Mesilla Valley in the south.

Chile has been in the New Mexican diet for generations. It was cultivated by the Incas, Mayas, and Aztecs, and may already have been a part of the Pueblo

Indian diet. With the arrival of Don Juan de Oñate, a merger of Hispanic, Mexican, and Indian foods began. Oñate's men were Spaniards, Creoles (sons of Spanish parents born in Mexico) and Mestizos (Aztec Indian or Mexican tribes mixed with Spanish blood), with a varied background of cooking habits. When they entered San Juan Pueblo in 1598, they had cattle, sheep, goats, chickens, pigs, wheat, chocolate, sugar, beans, garbanza, and other legumes to introduce to the Indians.

The San Juan shared their corn, squash, melons and wild turkeys with the newcomers, In turn, the colonizers taught the Indians how to use milk and wheat flour to make bread. This began a multiple culture society living on food that was an ingenious mixture of each heritage.

Today's New Mexican dishes have been handed down from generation to generation and the food is not strictly Spanish, nor Mexican, nor Indian, but a subtle blend that is genuinely New Mexican.[13]

Chile is high in the content of vitamins A and C and also contains significant amounts of thymine, riboflavin and niacin.

An Associated Press report from London suggests that chile might help ulcer sufferers. Studies have shown that eating chili peppers does not harm the stomach and may even help ulcers. Capsaicin, the hot stuff within peppers, is the element that wards off the damage. Scientists speculate that capsaicin stimulates nerve fibers in the stomach that release a hormone, which in turn increases blood flow and helps to protect the stomach from irritants. The most dramatic benefits will probably be found with pure capsaicin rather than spicy food.[14]

Cactus in the Albuquerque foothills.

**What is the most commonly asked question in Albuquerque restaurants?**

"Red or green?" If you answer, "Christmas chile" or "Christmas tree," it is understood that you want both.

**What was the Whittlesey House?**

A Norwegian log cabin in the heart of the Southwest, it is visible from I-25, south of Central. In 1903, owner/architect Charles Whittlesey built it for his family. Whittlesey was the architect of the city's Alvarado Hotel. The Albuquerque Press Club bought the property in 1973.[15]

**What are some of the historical places in Albuquerque that are said to be haunted?**

According to Antonio Garcez, in his book, *Adobe Angels (The Ghosts of Albuquerque)*, there have been recent sightings or evidence of 'ghosts' in places like The KiMo Theater, The Albuquerque Press Club, and the Maria Teresa Restaurant (formerly the Salvador Armijo House). Patrons and wait staff have seen people dressed in clothes not of this period, sometimes only in mirrors. Piano music is heard from a room where there is a piano, but no one in the room. This usually happens late at night when there are only a few employees left at the restaurant. Fixtures move, drop, or break and there is no logical explanation. The Luna Mansion, now a restaurant and only minutes away from Albuquerque, has been placed on the National Register of Historic Places. This fine restaurant, like the Maria Teresa, is said to be haunted by ghosts of the former owners. Patrons there have felt their hair pulled or been touched from behind by an unknown presence. Both restaurants are restored residences that have been filled with beautiful antiques and offer a great selection of dishes. These are reasons enough to visit these places and the rumor of 'ghosts' only adds to the richness of their histories.

**What are the five flags that are flown over Old Town, Albuquerque?**

Spain (1598-1821); Mexico (1821-1846); Confederate States (1862); USA (1846-present); and New Mexico (1912-present).

**What company is known as the original paranormal outfitter in the Land of Enchantment?**

New Mexico Ghost Tours conducts walking tours of Old Town every evening. The Ghost Walk of Old Town Albuquerque was featured on the Travel Channel's "Weird Travels, New Mexico's Visitors" in May of 2004. On the walking tour, guides give a rich narrative of the history of Old Town, as well as stories of recent hauntings and sightings of ghosts.

The information that the tour guides share comes from evidence gathered by members of the Southwest Ghost Hunter's Association during investigations of phenomena at various locations in Old Town, as well as other sites around the state. Ghosts can manifest as otherwise inexplicable energy fields measurable in shape and intensity with electromagnetic detectors. Tape recorders, infrared video cameras, and digital still cameras are also used.[16]

A ghost sighting is not guaranteed, but you never know.

Old Town during Ghost Tour.

**In 1706, what was Albuquerque's population?**

252.[17]

**What are those small, brown nuts that everyone makes such a fuss about?**

Piñon, or piñones, are those little brown nuts with an addicting flavor that we see sold on roadside stands in pound packages. The miniature cone which appears at the tip of new growth on pine trees early each summer does not develop into a mature one until the autumn of the second year. New Mexico is the heart of the commercially important piñon country, which extends to southern Colorado and eastern Arizona. These areas are the primary source of the Pinus edulis, the state tree of New Mexico.

Piñon nuts are known as the nut pine, the Colorado piñon or the pinyon pine. Long before piñones were marketed, they were bartered by the Indians and Spanish settlers. Coronado's exploration reports notes them in 1540. The trees grow at 5-9,000 feet and the average size is fifteen to thirty-five feet. Natives usually wait until the cones fall off the trees to pick the nuts. They are usually roasted in a very hot oven for ten to fifteen minutes for the best flavor. [18]

**What is the most recent addition to the city of Albuquerque that reflects its uniqueness and diversity, gaining national and international recognition?**

The opening of the National Hispanic Cultural Center of New Mexico, located in Albuquerque at Fourth and Bridge SW in the heart of the historic Barelas neighborhood. At the grand opening weekend, October 20-22, 2000, there were dignitaries from around the world. Spain's Crown Prince Felipe de Borbón and Edward Romero, a native Albuquerquean and the ambassador to Spain, both addressed the crowds on opening weekend. Vice President Al Gore dedicated the Center. In his speech, Senator Pete Domenici reminded the crowd that it was 22 years before the Pilgrims landed at Plymouth Rock in 1620, and it was nine years before the settlement of Jamestown in 1607, that Juan de Oñate arrived in New Mexico and founded the second city in North America, San Gabriel de los Espanoles.[19]

The National Hispanic Cultural Center is dedicated to the study, advancement, and presentation of Hispanic culture, arts, and humanities.

### Who are the Maloofs?

The Maloof Companies are a diversified group of business ventures including hotels, casinos, banking, food and beverage, and transportation headquartered in Albuquerque, New Mexico and operated in New Mexico, Colorado, and Nevada.

The Maloofs were the owners of the Houston Rockets from 1979 through 1982. Following the death of their father, George Maloof, Sr., in 1980, Joe and Gavin Maloof, who were only in their mid-20s at the time, took over responsibility for the Rockets along with their mother, Colleen, and brothers, George, Jr. and Phil, and sister, Adrienne.

The Maloofs now own the Sacramento Kings and Monarchs. Even more impressive than the company's competitive accomplishments has been the Maloof Sports and Entertainment's significant impact within the community of Sacramento. The Maloofs donate significant amounts of money each year to assist area capital improvement projects as a tribute to the family's late father and husband.

In 1994, the family made a $10 million investment in the Fiesta Casino Hotel in Las Vegas, Nevada. In 2000, the Maloofs sold the operating interest in the hotel for over $185 million and immediately re-invested the money into the construction of the Palms Hotel and Casino in Las Vegas.

In addition to their gaming business, the Maloofs have exclusive proprietorship rights to the distribution of Coors, Miller, Corona, Heineken, Tecate, InBev, Boston Beer, and Guinness products throughout New Mexico. The Maloof Companies also is one of the largest single shareholders in Wells Fargo Bank.

Colleen Maloof serves as Chair of the Board of Directors of the Maloof Companies.

The Maloof family history in the United States dates back to 1892 when Joe Maloof I opened a small general store in northern New Mexico. By the 1930s, the Maloof family acquired the distribution rights to Coors beer and subsequently established Quality Imports, a wholesale fine liquor distribution center, in 1937. When Joe Maloof I suffered a major heart attack in 1944, his son, George J. Maloof, left his studies at the University of Colorado to assume responsibility of the Maloof Companies at the age of 21. George J. Maloof successfully expanded the family business into a group of diversified companies, moving into the hotel and banking sectors in the 1970s.

The Maloofs are in the process of expanding their business in the entertainment industry with the development of Maloof Productions and Maloof Music.

For over 100 years, the Maloof family business philosophy has always been centered around customer and employee satisfaction.[20]

**What is Las Mañanitas?**

An historic landmark in Albuquerque at 1800 Rio Grande Boulevard NW, it is also a rare surviving mid-19$^{th}$ century adobe. All the features of the house are significant because they illustrate the history of the house through its owners. Residents of Duranes, the old farming community surrounding Las Mañanitas, remember that their grandparents recalled the days when the building was a stagecoach stop on the road through the valley to Santa Fe, called El Camino Real until the 1850s, then named the Chihuahua Trail. It also operated as a pool hall and a bar and many remember the dances or bailes held in the large living room. The Speronelli family owned the house and land at the turn of the century. The family owned a blacksmith shop and artifacts from the shop have been found on the property.[21]

**Where can Las Vegas style gaming be found in Albuquerque?**

At Sandia Resort & Casino on the Sandia Pueblo north of town and at Isleta Casino & Resort on the Pueblo of Isleta south of Albuquerque. Both have venues for entertainment and golf courses. Sandia boasts a hotel and spa as well.

**Is Albuquerque involved in international trade?**

Yes. The City of Albuquerque's Office of Economic Development established the International Trade Division in 2004. This Division helps Albuquerque companies sell goods and services in foreign markets. It also brings foreign investment into Albuquerque.

**What is the Frontier Restaurant?**

A restaurant that has served all of Albuquerque, but especially the University of New Mexico community, since 1971.

**What is a "Lobo"?**

"Lobo" is Spanish for wolf. It is UNM's mascot. George S. Bryan, a UNM student journalist in 1920, suggested the name. In an editorial for an issue of the UNM student newspaper, Bryan explained that the Lobo is "respected for his cunning, feared for his prowess, and is the leader of the pack."[22]

**Who makes Cheerios in Albuquerque?**

General Mills supply chain located in northwest Albuquerque.

**What famous author of numerous mystery novels that draw on Native American culture resides in Albuquerque?**

Tony Hillerman. Hillerman joined the journalism faculty of UNM in 1966. He taught there until 1987, serving as the department chair from 1976-81.

**Who is the courageous female leader whose name is synonymous with the civil rights movement in New Mexico?**

Alice Fay Kent Hoppes, who moved to Albuquerque in 1967. She was the voice of African American citizens in this community. She was president of the NAACP – Albuquerque Branch for 12 years. She led the efforts to create an African American Day at the annual State Fair. She was also instrumental in establishing a Martin Luther King state holiday. Alice Hoppes was appointed by Governor Bill Richardson in 2003 as director of the Office of African American Affairs. Among the many awards she received for her accomplishments was to be chosen one of the 1995 Outstanding New Mexico Women from the NM Commission on the Status of Women. Hoppes passed away in October of 2003 and, in 2004, Governor Richardson designated the African American Pavilion at the New Mexico State Fairgrounds, the "Alice Hoppes African American Pavilion."

**Who is the acclaimed Chicano writer who taught at the University of New Mexico before retiring in 1993?**

Rudolfo Anaya, who is best known for his award winning novels: *Bless Me Ultima* (1972), *Tortuga (1979),* and *Alburquerque* (1992).

Anaya says that he has always used the technique of the 'cuento.' He says that he is an oral storyteller, but puts it on the printed page.

**Who is Albuquerque's latest up and coming Latina author?**

Albuquerque Native Alisa Valdes-Rodriguez, Pulitzer Prize nominee. She has worked for the Boston Globe (where she was nominated for the Pulitzer) and the Los Angeles Times. Her first novel in 2003, *The Dirty Girls Social Club*, made her famous and introduced "Chica Lit," which is chick lit with Latina characters, according to Valdes-Rodriguez.[23] In 2005, Time Magazine dubbed her the "Godmother of Chica Lit" and named her one of the 25 most influential Hispanics in the United States. Alisa wrote the novel in a Starbucks on the west side of Albuquerque.

Valdes-Rodriguez received her bachelor's degree in saxophone performance from the Berklee College of Music. She earned a master's degree in journalism from Columbia University. Her father is a sociology professor at the University of New Mexico.

**Where do buffalo roam in Albuquerque?**

On land that belongs to Sandia Pueblo, you can spot the bison herd south of Tramway Road when heading west.

**How did Bueno Foods begin?**

As a small neighborhood grocery store, The Ace Food Store, on Bridge Street in 1946.[24] The Baca family started Bueno Foods in 1951. They were the first to flame roast green chile on a commercial scale. They had the idea of freezing freshly roasted green chile since the early 1950s when most households were buying freezers. Bueno Foods is still owned and operated by the Baca Family.

Buffalo grazing on open land south of Tramway Road.

**What prompted Bill Gates and Paul Allen to start Microsoft Corporation in Albuquerque in 1975?**

When Gates and Allen were fourteen years old, they were already writing and testing computer programs for fun and profit. As sophomores in college, they read in *Popular Mechanics* about the world's first commercially available microcomputer, MITS' 'softwareless' Altair 8800. The two created a new version of the BASIC computer language for the Altair. MITS bought their system and offered them office space in Albuquerque.[25]

In 1975, Gates and Allen founded the Microsoft Corporation in Albuquerque. Microsoft would sell its BASIC system to MITS, NCR and Intel. In 1979, Bill Gates moved Microsoft and its sixteen employees from Albuquerque to Seattle, Washington.[26]

# Entertainment and Fine Arts

**In the latter half of the nineteenth century, what two hotels were built and touted as the finest south of Denver and east of San Francisco?**

The Armijo House on Railroad Avenue (now Central Avenue) and the San Felipe on Gold Avenue.

**What impressive hotel, described as the most magnificent railroad hotel in the Fred Harvey chain, opened in Albuquerque in 1902?**

The Alvarado Hotel opened on May 11, 1902 under a blaze of electric lights. It was designed by architect Charles Whittlesey in a variation of Spanish or California Mission style architecture and decorated by Mary J. Colter, an authority on southwestern art, ethnology and archeology.

The Alvarado Hotel was impressive for its time. It boasted 89 rooms, a restaurant, bar, banquet facilities and parlors for men and women. Lawns were kept in immaculate condition, and passersby were requested to stay off the grass. A common pastime was to lunch at the Alvarado and relax on the promenade, watching for any important people who might come in on the afternoon trains.[27]

In 1970, the Alvarado was torn down to make room for a parking lot. In 2002, the Alvarado Transportation Center was built on the site. It was built to resemble the old landmark and was built as a replacement for the old train station, which burned in 1993. The station is a hub for all

Alvarado Hotel – veranda, 1908. Courtesy Colorado Historical Society (William H. Jackson Collection, WHJ16157) (cropped).

Alvarado Hotel, 1908. Courtesy Colorado Historical Society (William H. Jackson Collection, WHJ36785).

local buses, Greyhound buses, and the Rail Runner commuter line. It also serves as the downtown headquarters for the city's transit department.

**Before the first automobiles, what objects were decorated as floats for Albuquerque's parades?**

Freight wagons were turned into floats for parades in Albuquerque.

**Where was Albuquerque's first opera house?**

The first opera house was the Grant Opera House on the southwest corner of Railroad Avenue and Third Street. It opened on November 21, 1882, with a presentation of *H.M.S. Pinafore* presented by the Albuquerque Musical Dramatic Society.

**When did the first annual fair in Albuquerque begin to draw national attention to the city and to New Mexico?**

Almost as soon as the new community of Albuquerque began. Community leaders such as Elias Stover, Franz Huning and Jose Perea planned a series of annual fairs to draw national attention to the town and New Mexico. There was considerable rivalry between Santa Fe and Albuquerque. Some local boosters hoped that the fairs would make Albuquerque the territorial capital, instead of Santa Fe. The first territorial fair opened on October 3, 1881, at the new fairgrounds just north and west of the present day intersection of Central Avenue and Rio Grande Boulevard.[28]

**What was the theme of the first fair?**

"Civilization of the $19^{th}$ Century and Civilization of Prehistoric Times."[29]

**What was a big attraction at the Territorial Fair in the early 1900s?**

The "Casino," which never featured gambling. It was an indoor performance theater and hall.

**Why did the Territorial Fairs cease and what program provided for their return?**

The Territorial Fairs ceased during World War I. Although they were moved to several sites around town, the event was never successful again until the Works Progress Administration and other depression-period programs provided workmen and materials to build a new State Fair complex. It was built at its present location.[30]

**What is Expo New Mexico?**

It is the annual New Mexico State Fair, one of the largest in the country. It is held in Albuquerque for 17 days every September.

**What is the "KiMo"?**

The KiMo is an historical landmark as well as a theater. Located at 423 Central, the KiMo was completed on September 19, 1927. The first movie shown was a silent one: "Painting the Town." Film stars like Gloria Swanson, Ginger Rogers and Tom Mix visited the KiMo. Even Sally Rand came to perform with her famous feather fans.

The KiMo was named by Pablo Abeita, then governor of Isleta Pueblo. He won a monetary prize in a naming contest. KiMo means "King of its Kind."

The KiMo Theatre was the dream of Oreste Bachechi, an Italian immigrant, who came to the U.S. and Albuquerque in 1885. He set up a business in a tent near the railroad tracks. A year after the elaborate theatre was completed, Bachechi died and his sons took over the management.[31]

An official grand opening was held in September, 2000 after a fourteen-month renovation that cost $2 million. This is the KiMo's third renovation since a fire in 1961. In 1927, the KiMo's architecture was called "Pueblo Deco." The building is historic; since 1977, the KiMo has been on the prestigious National Register of Historic Places.[32]

**Can one hear symphony music in Albuquerque?**

Yes. Albuquerque is home to the New Mexico Symphony Orchestra, the official symphony orchestra for the state of New Mexico. The orchestra made its debut in Albuquerque in 1932 as the Albuquerque Civic Symphony. Half their performances a year take place at the University of New Mexico's Popejoy Hall. The other half take place in Albuquerque area neighborhoods, schools, in New Mexico communities served by the Orchestra's touring program, and at the Rio Grande Zoo.[33]

The KiMo Theatre, 419-423 Central Ave., 1930. Photographer Brooks Studio. The Albuquerque Museum Photoarchives, PA1978.151.859.

### What is the Albuquerque Biological Park?

The Albuquerque BioPark consists of the Rio Grande Zoo and the Albuquerque Aquarium and Rio Grande Botanic Garden. The zoo is located at 903 Tenth Street SW and the aquarium and botanic garden are located at 2601 Central Avenue NW.

### What is the National Atomic Museum?

Located in Albuquerque, the National Atomic Museum is the next best introduction to the nuclear age after the Bradbury Science Museum in Los Alamos. It traces the history of the top-secret Manhattan Project of the 1940s, starting with a copy of the letter written to President Franklin D. Roosevelt by Albert Einstein suggesting the possible development of an atomic bomb.

### Where is the world's longest aerial tramway located?

Right here in Albuquerque. The 2.7 mile aerial tramway can be reached from I-40 (Exit 167, take Tramway Blvd. north) or from I-25 (Exit 234, take Tramway Rd. east). The Sandia Peak Tramway stretches across Domingo Baca Canyon. The tram itself is an engineering marvel, but visitors come to see the view from the top: 11,000 square miles.

Tram approaching the top of Sandia Peak.

Tram ascending from base of the Sandia Mountains.

Constructed with the aid of helicopters, it was completed in 1966 at a cost of $2 million. The tram whisks visitors from its base at an elevation of 6,600 feet to the top of 10,378-foot Sandia Peak in less than twenty minutes.

The tram cars run daily; contact the office for hours of operation. Skiers can avoid the drive to Sandia Ski Area by taking the tram directly to the top of one of the ski lifts. Sandiago's restaurant is located at the base of the tram and the High Finance restaurant is located at the top.

**How many museums are located in Albuquerque?**

Twenty-four. Diverse and interesting, they are:

*Albuquerque Skateboard Museum* (inside Skate City Supply, it is the owner's collection of skateboards from pre-1970 to new), 294-6699, 1311 Eubank NE;

*Albuquerque Museum* (with extensive art history and Albuquerque history collections), 243-7255, 2000 Mountain Rd. NW;

*Anderson-Abruzzo Albuquerque International Balloon Museum*, 768-6020, 9201 Balloon Museum Drive NE (Alameda at Balloon Fiesta Park);

*Ernie Pyle Memorial Branch Library* (a branch of the Albuquerque/Bernalillo County Library, this national historic landmark in Albuquerque was once the home of Ernie Pyle and displays his memorabilia alongside library books), 256-2065, 900 Girard SE;

*Explora* (with hands-on learning experiences in art, science and technology), 224-8300, 1701 Mountain Rd. NW;

*J & R Vintage Automobile Museum*, 867-2881, 3650-A Highway 528, Rio Rancho;

*John Lewis' Antique Typewriter Museum* (a collection of antique typewriters that is housed inside Business Systems & Machines), 884-0600, 4805 Menaul NE;

*Museum of Turquoise*, 247-8650, 2107 Central Ave. NW;

*Museum of Archaeology and Biblical History*, 217-1330, 10110 Constitution NE;

*National Atomic Museum* (traces the development of the atomic bomb), 245-2137, 1905 Mountain Rd. NW;

*National Hispanic Cultural Center*, 246-2261, 1701 4th St. SW;

*New Mexico Activities Association Hall of Pride and Honor* (a nationally recognized museum dedicated to New Mexico's interscholastic activities), 923-3110, 6600 Palomas Ave. NE;

*New Mexico Holocaust and Intolerance Museum*, 247-0606, 415 Central Ave. NW;

*Rattlesnake Museum*, 242-6569, 202 San Felipe NW;

*Telephone Pioneer Museum of New Mexico*, 842-2937, 110 4th St. NW;

*The Indian Pueblo Cultural Center* (which features arts and crafts by nineteen Indian pueblos; and is also a good beginning before visiting the individual pueblos), 843-7270, 2401 12th St. NW;

*The New Mexico Museum of Natural History and Science*, 841-2800, 841-2802, the Lockheed Martin Dynatheater, and the Lodestar Astronomy Center, 841-5960, 1801 Mountain Rd. NW;

University of New Mexico Museums (six):

*The University Art Museum*, 277-4001, UNM Center for the Arts, Room 1017;

*Johnson Gallery*, 277-4967, 1909 Las Lomas NE;

*The Maxwell Museum of Anthropology* (with special emphasis on the cultural heritage of the Southwest), 277-4405, east of University, between Las Lomas and Dr. Martin Luther King Jr. Ave.;

*The Museum of Southwestern Biology*, 277-1360 (in the Department of Biology);

*The Geology Museum*, 277-4204, Northrop Hall, first floor; and

*The Meteorite Museum*, 277-2747, Northrop Hall, first floor;

*Unser Racing Museum*, 237-9094, 1776 Montano Rd. NW;

**What is Casa San Ysidro?**

Casa San Ysidro, The Gutierrez/Minge House, was donated to the Albuquerque Museum by Alan and Shirley Minge. The Minges had purchased the home in 1952 and spent more than 40 years collecting artifacts for it and restoring the original house, which dates to the 1870s. Their collection of artifacts was acquired by the Museum in 1997.

The Minges also built many more rooms onto the house around a central plazuela to recreate an $18^{th}$ century rancho. The house is located in the village of Corrales, across the road from the old San Ysidro Church. The church and house are named for the patron saint of farming, San Ysidro Labrador. Before the Minges acquired the property, it belonged to the descendants of Felipe Gutierrez, recipient of the Bernalillo Township grant in 1704.[34]

Guided tours are given daily of the house, except in December and January.

**What is Tinkertown Museum?**

A unique museum located on the Turquoise Trail National Scenic Byway on the way to Sandia Crest. This unique museum contains an animated miniature wood-carved Western town and a circus in a compound with walls made from glass bottles. Tinkertown (phone 281-5233) is open every day from April 1st through November 1st and is well worth the visit!

**What international event does Albuquerque host every October that is the most photographed in the world?**

The Albuquerque International Balloon Fiesta is held annually during the first two weekends of October. The Balloon Fiesta is the world's largest hot air balloon rally and brings together more than 1,000 colorful aerialists in races, "glow events," and contests. On each of the two weekends all the balloons are launched, weather permitting, starting at 7 a.m., in a spectacular mass ascension. Balloon Fiesta Park is located on Alameda Blvd. NE, just west of Interstate 25.

**When did Albuquerque host the first International Balloon Fiesta?**

In 1972. There were thirteen balloons and they launched from the Coronado Shopping Center's parking lot. Since 1972, increasing numbers of balloons have flown at the fiesta. Official records on balloon registration are:

| Year | # of Balloons |
|---|---|
| 1972 | 13 |
| 1973 | 138 |
| 1974 | 111 |
| 1975 | 170 |
| 1976 | 153 |
| 1977 | 194 |
| 1978 | 273 |
| 1979 | 360 |
| 1980 | 312 |
| 1981 | 492 |
| 1982 | 447 |
| 1983 | 469 |
| 1984 | 476 |
| 1985 | 476 |
| 1986 | 485 |
| 1987 | 517 |
| 1988 | 600 |
| 1989 | 500 (limited registration) |
| 1990 | 602 |
| 1991 | 632 |
| 1992 | 646 |
| 1993 | 653 |
| 1994 | 650 |
| 1995 | 671 |

| Year | # of Balloons |
|---|---|
| 1996 | 850 |
| 1997 | 841 |
| 1998 | 873 |
| 1999 | 903 |
| 2000 | 1,019 |
| 2001 | 770 |
| 2002 | 722 |
| 2003 | 719 |
| 2004 | 741[35] |
| 2005 | 700[36] |

According to the 2005 Balloon Fiesta final statistics, there were 41 states and 18 countries registered to fly.

**How much do hot air balloons cost?**

New balloons start at around $20,000 for the smaller one that carries one person in addition to the pilot. Larger balloons that carry 2-3 passengers in addition to the pilot range between $20,000 - $30,000. Special shapes, or balloons with custom features are priced higher. Used balloons are available occasionally.[37]

**What were Albuquerque's first radio stations?**

KKOB, AM radio (770 on the dial) first broadcast to Albuquerque on April 5, 1922 from Las Cruces, then moved to Albuquerque in October of 1982. However, the first

Hot air balloon with Zia symbol floating over the river and bosque. Photograph courtesy of Marble Street Studio, Inc.

station to broadcast from Albuquerque did so in a truck equipped with a mobile studio, transmitter, and tower. It was KGGM at 610 on the dial. Albuquerque's first FM station, KANW (tuned at 89.1) began on September 11, 1950. With its 350 watt transmitter, it had educational programming and no commercials. The first commercial FM station, KHFM (tuned at 96.3) began broadcasting on October 8, 1954.

### What was Albuquerque's first TV station?

KOB-TV began broadcasting on November 29, 1948. George S. Johnson, from KOB radio, became the first station manager.

# Ancient Albuquerque

**How far into the past do the roots of Albuquerque's Old Town extend?**

Old Albuquerque, the West End, or Old Town, was a community with roots dating back to the early 17$^{th}$ century. The first farms and ranches were established in the area (about 1610 to 1630) by families such as those of Trujillo, Chavez, and Caravajal.

**What did archaeological excavations at Sandia Cave determine about when the earliest humans had been there?**

Beginning in 1936, a series of archaeological excavations was carried out at Sandia Cave, on the north end of the Sandia Mountains. When layers of deposit were stripped away, one lower level of material demonstrated, conclusively, that man had used the cave as a shelter 10,000 years before.

**What was the first church established in Albuquerque?**

The first church in Albuquerque was San Felipe de Neri (named for the saint, San Felipe Neri) in Old Town. The Franciscans built the original church on the west side of

San Felipe de Neri Church in Old Town on Church St., 1885.
The Albuquerque Museum Photoarchives, PA1978.50.37.

the plaza in 1705-1706. They rebuilt it on its present site about 1793. The priests served a larger geographical area than the plaza by riding a circuit to outlying chapels and performing services, such as weddings, baptisms and burials. There were some Protestant services performed in Old Town before the arrival of the railroad, but the majority of residents were Catholic.

**What area was known as Ranchos de Albuquerque?**

A cluster of farms between Sandia's southern boundary and the northern limits of the villa. The lands of this community had been granted initially to Captain Diego Montoya by Governor Peñuela in 1712. They were conveyed shortly afterward to Elena Gallegos, the widow of Santiago Gurule. The property that eventually became known as the Elena Gallegos grant amounted to an estimated 70,000 acres.

Much of the land was situated on the East Mesa and in the Sandia Mountains. Ranchos de Albuquerque was only one of several little settlements that took root on the Elena Gallegos grants. In most settlements were single extended families which gave their name to the settlement, in keeping with Spanish custom: Los Griegos, Los Montoyas, Los Poblanos, and Los Gallegos.

**What formerly existed on the site upon which Albuquerque would be founded in 1706?**

By the middle 1660s, there existed about 45 estates in the entire valley. The main houses on these properties were referred to as haciendas.[38]

Romero Street in Old Town looking South, 1885. The Albuquerque Museum Photoarchives, PA1980.31.1.

Unidentified residence, exterior, unidentified men, Old Town, 1895. The Albuquerque Museum Photoarchives, PA1990.13.228.

**Who claimed responsibility for calling and naming the villa on the banks of the Rio Grande (then known as the Rio del Norte) "Alburquerque"?**

On April 23, 1706, seventy years before the American Revolution, Governor Francisco Cuervo y Valdéz of New Mexico composed a formal document to his sovereign in Spain and to the viceroy in Mexico City, attesting to the creation of a new town:

'I certify to the king, our lord, and the most excellent señor viceroy: That I founded a villa on the banks and in the valley of the Rio del Norte in a good place as regards land, water, pasture, and firewood. I gave it as patron saint the glorious apostle of the Indies, San Francisco Xavier, and called and named it the villa of Alburquerque.'[39]

Governor Cuervo asserted that 35 families had already taken up residence in the town (252 adults and children). He added that a church had been completed and a house for the priest was under way.

**How did the governor justify the legality of his actions?**

The governor declared that he had followed the procedure prescribed for the establishment of new municipalities as set forth in the royal laws contained in the Recopilación de Leyes de los Reynos de las Indias, Spain's monumental compilation of laws. The Recopilación covered practically all the aspects of colonial government and public life; one section dealt specifically with the procedures and requirements necessary for the creation of new towns.[40]

**What is known about the town of Alburquerque in Spain?**

In Spain the town of Alburquerque (spelled with the extra 'r') is located in the province of Badajoz, close to the Portuguese border. It contains an impressive castle, which is the traditional home of the Dukes of Alburquerque.

Its original name was albaquercus in Roman times, which derives from the Latin *albus quercus*, meaning "white oak." The municipal coat of arms bears a single white oak on a crimson field.[41]

**What infectious disease was common from the days of earliest settlement?**

Smallpox, a feared and deadly infectious disease. The Spanish folk called it 'el peste.' In 1798, Englishman Edward Jenner had discovered an effective vaccine. The Spanish King equipped an expedition to sail around the world to each of its colonies and distribute the vaccine. Some of Albuquerque's children began to be vaccinated in 1804.

**What account of Albuquerque was given by one of the first Americans to visit and be briefly detained and questioned in Santa Fe for breaking the Spanish law against trespassers?**

That of Lieutenant Zebulon Pike. His account was that the Spaniards were a model of courtesy. After being questioned in Santa Fe by Governor Joaquin Real Alencaster, he was dined in the old mud palace. Pike said that it was not like captivity at all and the Americans were allowed to keep their personal possessions, including side arms. They were allowed to explore the streets of the capital.

In March, 1807, Pike and his men, on military escort to Chihuahua City, stopped in Albuquerque.

The people of the middle valley were at work clearing the irrigation ditches in preparation for spring planting. Pike recalled that the cultivation of the fields was a joyful labor done by men, women, and children. His account provides us with the first reference to colonial Albuquerque by an American visitor. In Mexico, Pike's written account was taken from him and from memory, he assembled a report of his experiences, which was published in 1810. This work gave Americans their first view of Hispanic life and customs on the Rio Grande.

**What was life like for a typical Albuquerque family in the early 1800s?**

In the typical rancho, one would find the women grinding their own grain (which was stored throughout the home in huge chests), making their own bread or tortillas, and cooking from sunrise to sunset, while washing dishes, pots, and pans in between. The women helped their husbands take care of the farm animals when he was away trading on the Santa Fe Trail. When the men were away, typically for weeks at a time, the women were in charge of protecting home and family from the incessant Indian raids that took place in early Albuquerque all throughout the 1700s and up until 1850. The women knew how to use a shotgun and would not hesitate to do so. There were some women in the village who were curanderas (healers) and were called on to tend to the sick on a regular basis. There were also those that were the village's midwives, as well. When the men were away, the women also had to chop wood for the fire, or at times, even take the horse and cart to get more wood.

Most of the Spanish homes of this period had very little furniture. There were few chairs to sit on and the only table was used for preparing food, usually. There might have been one bed in the home. Sometimes, many people lived in a few rooms. The bathroom was an outhouse and some family member had the chore of emptying the chamber pot every morning. Most homes had an altar of some sort; some even had a small chapel with an altar and santos (statues of saints) displayed.

**What is the earliest known building along Central Avenue that is still in use today?**

The Manzano Day School, located just to the east of Old Town, at 1801 Central Avenue NW. La Glorieta, the house at the heart of Manzano Day School is on the National Register of Historic Places. The original house was built around 1662 by Don Diego de Trujillo as the Trujillo Casa Del Estancia, El Bosque Grande. La Glorieta was once the home of Manuel Armijo, governor of the state for Mexico in the 1830s and 1840s.[42]

La Glorieta served as headquarters to Confederate soldiers during the Civil War in 1862. The hacienda and 700 acres of land were purchased from Franciscan Friars by Franz Huning in 1882. Huning was a German immigrant that owned a general store in Old Town. As his store prospered, he added west and north wings, forming a courtyard, and named the house La Glorieta. La Glorieta means bower or arbor. When Huning moved into Huning Castle, he gave La Glorieta to his daughter as a wedding present.[43]

Huning's granddaughter, Erna Fergusson, was born at La Glorieta. Erna Fergusson became a well known author who went on to write books about Albuquerque and New Mexico.

Manzano Day School was founded in 1938 by Ruth Simms. She was an Illinois Congresswoman who moved to New Mexico after she married Albert G. Simms, a one-time Republican U.S. House member.

# Albuquerque at the Turn of the Century

**When did Albuquerque incorporate as a town? As a city?**

In 1885, Albuquerque incorporated as a town and, in 1891, as a city.

**Was Albuquerque ethnically diverse at the turn of the century?**

Yes. The 1900 U.S. Census records more than 26 groups ranging from Chinese to English, and from Hispanic to Russian. The population in 1900 was 6,026 persons (excluding Old Town), and the largest ethnic/racial group in New Town was Hispanic, with 906 persons, or 15% of the total. Other large first generation groups were the Germans, African-Americans, Canadians and English.

**By the turn of the century, what were the names of some of the old families of Albuquerque as well as the newcomers then who have remained until the present generation?**

The old families were the Armijos, Bacas, Chavezes, Duranes, Espinosas, Garcias, Gutierrezes, Montoyas, Oteros, Padillas, Sanchezes, Yrisarris, and Zamoras and were joined by the families such Blueher, Everitt, Hubbell, Hughes, Huning, Mann, McClellan, McGuinness, Metzgar, Ross,

View of San Felipe Church, rectory and corner of Plaza in Old Town, 1918. Photographer William Walton. The Albuquerque Museum Photoarchives, PA1994.14.53.

Rutherford, Springer, Staehlin, Stamm, Strong and Stover. Other early family names include Bachechi, Borradaile, Cobb, Easterday, Fergusson, Ilfeld, Kaseman, Keleher, Korber, Lembke, Mandell, Matteucci, Rodey, With, and many more.

**When did the railroad come to Albuquerque?**

April 22, 1880.

**What do photographs taken between 1880 and 1900 reveal about the city that Albuquerque was?**

The best concept of the appearance of the city can be gained from the birdseye views taken between 1880 and 1900. The photographs reveal a compact, industrialized city of about 7,000 centered around the railroad with a few outlying residential districts. There was little construction east of Arno Street or west of Sixth Street.

**What were some of the reasons that New Mexico appealed to Easterners as a place to live?**

Albuquerque's Commercial Club, about 1883, issued strong appeals to persons in the East suffering from respiratory illnesses, especially tuberculosis. At first, the claims promised virtually instant recovery from almost any ailment.

> Persons with weak lungs, or with
> a tendency to consumption, may count
> that they will never fall a
> victim to the dread destroyer

> if they take up residency here.
> Bronchitis, chronic pneumonia,
> chronic malaria, hay fever and
> general debility are among the
> diseases that are almost surely
> cured in this climate.
>
> \- *Plain Statements Regarding New Mexico, 1893*

By the turn of the century, Albuquerque witnessed a flood of health seekers, many terminally ill and with no financial resources. When they became a burden on local charitable organizations, booster booklets were revised to discourage any newcomers who arrived with no money or possessions.

> To those without means of subsistence,
> with only the price of a ticket, we
> say do not come. Our people are full
> of charity for the afflicted, but there
> is a limit to their means; they must
> first provide for their own.
>
> \- *Albuquerque Illustrated, 1900*

Many of Albuquerque's citizens moved here because of respiratory ailments. Clyde Tingley arrived because of his wife's illness. Clinton P. Anderson came in on the Santa Fe expecting to die shortly. Carrie Tingley recovered and founded a children's hospital in Hot Springs, now Truth or Consequences. Anderson became a U.S. Senator and leading businessman.[44]

**Who was the founder of the Rio Grande Zoological park?**

In 1923, the zoo started out with a pair of mountain lions, said to have been captured in either the Sandia or Manzano Mountains, according to the Rio Grande Zoo. (According to Albuquerque Museum accounts, some animals had been collected earlier from a circus passing through town and the idea belonged to Clyde Tingley.)

In 1927, the zoo was given a monkey, called Friday, by Douglas Fairbanks and Mary Pickford. This monkey had been in the move, 'Robinson Crusoe.'

In 1972, the Zoological society banquet was held to celebrate the arrival of the rhinos and featured alligator tails hors d'oeuvres, frozen from the previous year's winter death. A bond issue, passed in 1975, paid for the construction of the Reptile House and the Rain Forest.

**Who was responsible for much of Albuquerque's architecture?**

A former New Yorker, a Columbia University graduate, Edward Buxton Cristy, who drew up plans for the Barnett Block at Second and Central, for Hadley Hall and other university buildings, Central School, the Presbyterian, Episcopal and Methodist churches and most of the finer residences in the city.

**How would Albuquerque residents from 1883 to 1955 remember "Castle Huning"?**

Franz Huning was a merchant and developer in Albuquerque. He built Castle Huning, a massive home, as a

Christmas present for his family in 1883. The house was located on a 700 acre estate called Rancho Seco on the south side of the intersection of Railroad Avenue and Fifteenth Street. The house was built of red sod bricks which were sheathed in wood and carved to imitate brick. Castle Huning was demolished in 1955 for a construction project which was never realized.[45]

**What is Franz Huning's connection with the present day High Noon Restaurant & Saloon in Old Town?**

His descendants were owners of this property at different times. The building of the High Noon Saloon in which the foyer and Santo room are located was constructed in 1785. It is one of the original structures in historic Old Town. In 1884, the building was sold to Lucian and Juanita Huning Duran. Leonardo Huning was the owner from 1887 to 1894.

The building is said to have also occupied a gambling casino and a popular brothel.

**Was there a problem with air pollution in Albuquerque around the turn of the century?**

Pictures taken between 1880 and 1900 reveal that air pollution from coal smoke was heavy, but street traffic was usually light.

Huning Castle, 1910. The Albuquerque Museum Photoarchives, PA1980.154.25.

**When were military aircraft flown to Albuquerque for storage?**

Following World War II.

**A highlight of the year 1909 was the visit by what President to Albuquerque?**

President William Howard Taft. At the time, all of New Mexico was promoting a campaign for Statehood and the political leaders hoped the visit would aid the cause.

**Who owned Albuquerque's first automobile?**

Mr. R.L. Dodson, a bicycle dealer, was the first to drive in Albuquerque during November of 1897. The vehicle was a wire-spoked "Locomobile."

By 1910, there were 32 automobiles, also called "buzz wagons" or "Devil Wagons" by irate horse riding citizens. Only two years later, in 1912, there were 911 automobiles registered in New Mexico.

**What is the origin of Tingley Beach?**

A city dump, an eyesore at the edge of Rio Grande Park and Zoo. Mayor Clyde Tingley worked out a deal with the Middle Rio Grande Conservancy District to rearrange its levees and divert water in the small lake. It was first known as Conservancy Beach, later named Ernie Pyle Beach and often called Tingley Beach. After several years, swimming was prohibited because of health hazards.

1897 Locomobile owner R.L. Dodson, 1910. The Albuquerque Museum Photoarchives, PA1990.13.240.

**What was the name of the "best known" saloon at the turn of the century?**

According to author Erna Fergusson, it was the White Elephant. Saloons were abundant then, about four to every block. The White Elephant, for many years, was a recognized institution of the Southwest, whose reputation was based on the absolute honesty of the games, its magnificence and superior taste, and its "hand-oil painting" of naked ladies. The solid mahogany bar and fixtures cost twelve thousand dollars and the bar was so long that fifty men could put their feet on the rail at one time. Play was so high that one night, twenty-four thousand dollars was taken in at the tables. On one different night, a man from Denver won eleven thousand dollars.[46]

**What type of homes could one find in the new developments and how did these homes compare with adobe homes?**

Before the railroad arrived in Albuquerque, the Territorial style of adobe construction was prevalent due to the scarcity of bricks and milled lumber. The new developments included frame and brick homes in Gothic, Queen Anne and Italianate styles with touches of 'gingerbread' woodwork and elaborate brickwork. These new homes were attractive, but adobe houses with their thick courses of adobe bricks were cooler in the summer and warmer in the winter.[47]

**Why did the Albuquerque Gas and Electric Company change its name to Public Service Company of New Mexico?**

On May 1, 1917, Albuquerque Gas and Electric started doing business in New Mexico. It changed its name almost two decades later to reflect its operations across the state.

**When was the Albuquerque Convention Center opened in downtown Albuquerque?**

In 1972, as part of the Urban Renewal program. The first facility manager was Jack Baker, father to John Baker.

# Albuquerque Politics and Politicians

**What group of men were known as the "merchant police"?**

New Albuquerque was under the jurisdiction of the Bernalillo County Sheriff in the beginning. The town marshal was appointed by the sheriff and the merchants often paid for the marshal's services. The marshal and his deputies were known as "merchant police."

**What U.S. President addressed the people of Albuquerque near the Alvarado Hotel about 1913?**

Theodore Roosevelt.

**What made the Alvarado the social and political center of Albuquerque for several decades?**

"Young men and women courted at the yearly Montezuma Ball, veterans of the Civil and Spanish American wars held reunions in the meeting rooms, President Theodore Roosevelt spoke to crowds from the courtyard, and in 1911, the New Mexico State Constitution was approved in the Alvarado banquet hall.

Competition for the Alvarado came in the 1920-1930s when motels and hotels sprang up downtown along routes 66 and 85. After the war, rail travel declined and the town expanded. The Alvarado was demolished (after many attempts to save it) for a parking lot in 1970."[48]

**Who was Elfego Baca?**

He was a sheriff at the time of the turn of the century, gaining publicity in movies, radio and literature. His claim to fame was the gunfight at Reserve, then San Francisco, in which he held off eighty angry cowboys in a gun battle that lasted thirty-six hours. He claimed to have met Billy the Kid at age sixteen and to have gone on rowdy escapades with him.

Baca was also a clerk in a country store, mayor of Socorro, county school superintendent, assistant district attorney, special agent for the cattlemen's association, miner, prospector, and real estate agent.

At one time he was an American representative for Pancho Villa, revolutionist, attorney for General Jose Ynez Salazar (wanted by Pancho Villa, who offered thirty thousand pesos for his capture), private detective, publisher and editor, and politician.

In 1911, he ran for the Senate and lost. In 1905 and 1906 he served as district attorney of Socorro County. As deputy, he is reputed to have killed seven men in stand-up fights. He had come to Albuquerque in 1910 to make his way as a lawyer and private detective.

It is said that, dressed in a flowing cape and trailed by a bodyguard, he stalked the downtown streets, handing out his business cards. Not so unusual, perhaps, but his business cards read on one side, "Elfego Baca, Attorney-at-Law, Fees Moderate," and on the reverse, "Private Detective; Divorce Investigations Our Specialty, Discreet Shadowing Done."

There are dozens of stories about Elfego's rare antics, particularly his performances while serving as an attorney in court. He is said to have definitely lent color to Albuquerque's political scene.

Elfego Baca handing hat to Eddie Mack, 1930. Photographer Brooks Studio. The Albuquerque Museum Photoarchives, PA1978.151.99.

**Who was called the "Runaway Governor" of New Mexico?**

Manuel Armijo of Albuquerque. On May 11, 1846, President James K. Polk went before Congress and read a formal Declaration of War with Mexico. New Mexico was a Mexican territory at the time. Manuel Armijo was in the midst of this third term as governor. He issued patriotic appeals to the population so that they would be ready at the first sign of American invasion.

An army was on its way from Fort Leavenworth, Kansas under the command of General Stephen Watts Kearny. Kearny's men knew of Manuel Armijo by reputation; his mistreatment of Texas prisoners in 1841 and his high-handed dealings with some of the Santa Fe traders.

When Armijo learned that Kearny's troops had occupied Las Vegas and were en route to the capital, he announced that he was withdrawing, giving up the game. He climbed into his American built carriage and headed for Mexico. He forgot to make a side trip to Albuquerque to bid his wife, Trinidad, goodbye.

Armijo did send word home, apparently, for he was joined by wagons bearing his personal possessions and other merchandise, but no wife. At the same time, a British adventurer, George Ruxton, was heading toward New Mexico from Chihuahua. Ruxton said he spoke briefly with the "Runaway Governor of New Mexico," then headed in to Albuquerque. There, Ruxton recounts, the Americans were not greeted with any hostility. Instead, the people of Albuquerque seemed pleased with the change of government and they said that Armijo had gone to the devil.

Manuel Armijo residence in Old Town. The Albuquerque Museum Photoarchives, PA1980.152.3.

**What decade brought about political and social change in Albuquerque at the same time witnessing the coming of the Anglo population to settle here?**

Probably the decade beginning in 1850. In a quarter century time span, Albuquerqueans had been transferred from the rule of Spain to that of Mexico, and, finally to the United States. Kearny's conquest of 1846 marked the beginning of the Americanization of Albuquerque. In 1851, New Mexico was organized as a territory. Now, the Hispanos, descendants all of Albuquerque's colonial families were no longer quite the masters in their own house. The effects of the coming of the Anglos were beginning to be felt in the Middle Valley. In the 1850s, Anglo merchants and developers were drawn to Albuquerque by the minor business boom which arose from increased military activity.

**How did the position of town marshal come about?**

In 1889, the town marshal became an elected officer and served a one-year term. Albuquerque was a rowdy and violent frontier town in its early years. Consequently, between 1881 and 1889, 26 men served as town marshals.

**Who was New Albuquerque's first town marshal and why was he hanged?**

A tall, slim, illiterate man who went by the name of Milt Yarberry, although those who have studied his life doubt this was his real name. He was in his early 30s and got the marshal's job because he was available and probably because of his reputation as a gunfighter. Not much else qualified him or was known about him.

Yarberry was hanged in Old Town in 1883 after shooting two men to death shortly after he became marshal and within three months of each other. The first man he killed shortly after becoming marshal was his rival for a certain woman's affections. Witnesses say that the man, Harry Brown, did initiate the verbal fight, however, all shots were fired by Yarberry, two or three of them after Brown was already down. Yarberry said at trial that Brown had been going for his gun when he shot him. Yarberry was acquitted.

The second man Yarberry killed was while he and a friend were investigating a shot being fired around the vicinity of First Street and Railroad Avenue. The man shot down was Charles Campbell, a railroad carpenter described as a quiet man, a loner. Someone had pointed out Campbell to Yarberry as the person who fired the shot. Campbell was shot three times, twice in the back. Yarberry said that Campbell had shot at him five or six times, but the problem was that Campbell's gun was nowhere to be found and no one knew for sure if he was the one who fired the shot that started the investigation.

While Yarberry was held in the Santa Fe jail awaiting trial, he escaped. He was captured a few days later. He returned to Albuquerque on February 9, 1883 for his execution at the Bernalillo County Jail, east of the Plaza in Old Town. One hundred people had bought tickets to view the hanging; hundreds more viewed it from tree and roof tops.

When the noose was put on Yarberry's neck, he was asked if he had anything to say. He talked for fifteen minutes and was still talking when the black hood was slipped over his head, claiming his innocence. The gallows was a new design then, that yanked the hanging victim upwards when the 325-pound weight was dropped.[49]

This explains why Milt Yarberry was buried with the hanging rope still around his neck. He was buried in Mt. Calvary Cemetery in the Santa Barbara plot area. Rumor has it that his ghost haunts the cemetery and can be seen from the front gates off of Edith Street. Those who have seen the ghost later find out that it is Yarberry when they describe the rope around the man's neck that moves from side to side when he walks.

**Who was the first mayor of Albuquerque?**

The first mayor of Albuquerque was Henry Jaffa, a merchant. Until 1898, city officials served one-year terms, which were expanded to two-year terms in 1899 and to four-year terms in 1904.

**What did Albuquerque Mayors Henry Jaffa and Harry Kinney have in common?**

They both spent the formative periods of their lives in Trinidad, Colorado.

**Who was Edmund G. Ross?**

A Kansas senator whose vote saved President Andrew Jackson from being impeached and who later became the territorial governor of New Mexico. He was featured in the book, *Profiles in Courage*, by John F. Kennedy. He retired in Albuquerque and is buried here.

**What type of city government does Albuquerque have?**

The mayor-council form. The commission-manager form was the type of government used until the 1974 charter revision. In June, 1974, Albuquerque elected its first city officials under this new form of government. Under the Albuquerque Municipal Charter, the mayor is a full-time paid chief executive elected for a four-year term. He/she is assisted as head of administration by a chief administrative officer appointed by the mayor and confirmed by the council.

The mayor is responsible for the preparation and execution of the city budget. The nine-member council, elected by districts, serves staggered, four-year terms. Members serve part-time. The council is a legislative body. It prepares ordinances, rules and regulations for city government. It also proposes charter revisions.

**Who was the first female district court judge in Albuquerque?**

Mary Walters was the first female to serve as a district court judge in the District Court of the Second Judicial District of New Mexico. She served from July 6, 1971 through December 7, 1972.

**Who was the first city councilwoman in Albuquerque?**

Sondra L. Cohn West, who was the first and only woman among the first elected city council in Albuquerque in 1974.

**Who were Albuquerque's mayors, their trades and the years of their terms from 1885 to the present?**

| NAME | TRADE | TERM |
|---|---|---|
| Henry Jaffa | Grocer | 1885-86 |
| George Lail | Meat market speculator | 1886-87 |
| William Childers | Attorney | 1887-88 |
| Arthur E. Walker | Grocer, insurance | 1888-89 |
| Col. Gordon W. Meylert | Hotel owner | 1889-90 |
| Michael Mandell | Hardware and dry goods | 1890-91 |
| Joseph Exum Saint | Mining broker, rancher | 1891-92 |
| Dr. George Easterday | Physician | 1892-93 |
| Neill B. Field | Attorney | 1893-94 |
| John F. Luthy | Banker | 1894-95 |
| Joseph C. Baldridge | Lumber dealer | 1895-97 |

| NAME | TRADE | TERM |
|---|---|---|
| Dr. Strickland Aubright | Physician | 1897-98 |
| Frank W. Clancy | Attorney | 1898-99 |
| Owen N. Marron | Attorney, banker | 1899-1902 |
| Charles F. Meyers | Typographer, hardware | 1902-04 |
| Frank McKee | Bank cashier | 1904-08 |
| Felix H. Lester | Attorney | 1908-10 |
| Dr. John W. Elder | Physician | 1910-12 |
| Col. D.K.B. Sellers | Realtor | 1912-14 |
| David H. Boatright | Tire dealer | 1914-16 |
| Henry Westerfield | Cigar maker | 1916-17 |
| Charles F. Wade | Lumber manager | 1917-19 |

No official mayor was elected from 1916 to 1974. During those years, the City Commission Chairman served as ex-officio mayor.

| NAME | TRADE | TERM |
|---|---|---|
| Walter M. Connell | Sheep and wool dealer | 1919-22 |
| William R. Walton | Coal and lumber dealer | 1922* |
| Edwin B. Swope | Railroad electrician | 1923-25 |
| Clyde K. Tingley | Politician | 1925-34 |
| Charles H. Lembke | Contractor | 1935-38 |
| Clyde D. Oden | Car dealer | 1938-39 |
| Clyde K. Tingley | Politician | 1939-46 |
| Albert E. Buck | Steel plant chief | 1946-47 |
| Frank W. Darrow | Unknown | 1947* |
| Clyde K. Tingley | Politician | 1947-48 |
| Ernest E. Everly | Contractor | 1948-51 |
| Clyde K. Tingley | Politician | 1951-54 |

* Represents a term that was less than twelve months of that year.

| NAME | TRADE | TERM |
|---|---|---|
| Maurice Sanchez | Attorney | 1954-62 |
| Archie Westphall | School supplies dealer | 1962-66 |
| Ralph S. Trigg | Unknown | 1966-67 |
| Pete V. Domenici | Attorney | 1967-70 |
| Charles Barnhart | Attorney | 1970-71 |
| Harry Kinney | Mechanical engineer | 1971-73 |
| Louis E. Saavedra | TVI President | 1973* |
| Ray Baca | Policeman | 1973-74 |
| Richard G. Vaughn | Unknown | 1974* |
| Harry Kinney | Mechanical engineer | 1974-77 |
| David Rusk | Labor administrator | 1977-81 |
| Harry Kinney | Mechanical engineer | 1981-85 |

* Represents a term that was less than twelve months of that year.

| NAME | TRADE | TERM |
|---|---|---|
| Ken Schultz | Car dealer ownership | 1985-89 |
| Louis E. Saavedra | TVI President | 1989-93 |
| Martin Chavez | Attorney | 1993-97 |
| Jim Baca | Former TV news anchorman, elected official, and Director of the Bureau of Land Management | 1997-2001 |
| Martin Chavez | Attorney | 2001-Present |

* Represents a term that was less than twelve months of that year.

**How did Mayor Martin Chavez make history when he was re-elected in 2005?**

He was the first mayor to win consecutive terms since the city charter system began in 1974.

**What is unique about the New Mexico Constitution, which was approved at the Alvarado Hotel in Albuquerque in 1911?**

President William Howard Taft signed the bill admitting New Mexico as the 47th state, only after the state presented to him a state-approved constitution. The Constitution went into effect in 1912, but was drafted in 1910. Not only is it one of the longest documents among those of the other 49 states (over 21,000 words), but this document has significant provisions that protect the rights of Hispanics.

In addition, the features that protect Hispanics were intended to be "unamendable" by the founding fathers. Unamendable, meaning that it would take a proposal by three-fourths of the state legislature and be ratified by three-fourths of the voters in the state, with each county ratifying by two-thirds majority. This feat would be near impossible in some Northern New Mexico counties that are largely Hispanic, overwhelmingly Democratic, and whose roots go back over four hundred years. Sections of the Articles of these significant provisions are as follows:

*II. Bill of Rights*

The rights, privileges and immunities, civil, political and religious, guaranteed to the people of New Mexico by the Treaty of Guadalupe Hidalgo shall be preserved inviolate. (sec. 5)

*VII. Elective Franchise*

The right of any citizen of the State to vote, hold office, or sit upon juries, shall never be restricted, abridged or impaired on account of religion, race, language, or color, or inability to speak, read or write the English or Spanish languages, except as may otherwise be provided in this constitution . . .(sec. 3)

*XII. Education*

The legislature shall provide for the training of teachers in the normal schools or otherwise so that they may become proficient in both the English and Spanish languages ...

Children of Spanish descent in the State of New Mexico shall never be denied the right and privilege of admission and attendance in the publish schools or other public educational institutions …, and they shall never be classed in separate schools …, and the legislature shall provide penalties for the violation of this section. (sec. 10)

*XX. Miscellaneous*

For the first twenty years after this constitution goes into effect all laws passed by the legislature shall be published in both the English and Spanish languages. (sec. 12)

**What Albuquerque Catholic school was attended by Senator Pete Domenici of New Mexico?**

He graduated from St. Mary's High School in 1950. Senator Domenici was born in Albuquerque on May 7, 1932. He earned an education degree at the University of New Mexico in 1954. He was a Math teacher at Garfield Junior High School before becoming an attorney. Before becoming a teacher, Domenici pitched for the Albuquerque Dukes. He was first elected to office in 1972. Senator Domenici is the first New Mexican elected to serve six full six-year terms in the Senate.

**Who is Ed Romero?**

Former U.S. Ambassador to Spain, Edward L. Romero, who resides in Albuquerque, was appointed by President Clinton in 1998. During the Carter administration, he served on the federal advisory committee for trade negotiations and he was a member of the U.S. delegation to the Helsinki Accords.[50] Romero has also been a successful businessman; he was founder, chairman and chief executive officer of Advanced Sciences, Inc., an international environmental engineering and waste management company. This company merged with Commodore Applied Technologies in 1998. Romero also founded and serves on the board of directors of Valor Telecommunications Southwest LLC and RTM International, a Spanish company.[51]

Romero is a founder of the Hispanic Culture Foundation and the National Hispanic Cultural Center in New Mexico. In 2003, he was appointed to the Bank of America Corporation board of directors. Approximately 75% of the U.S. Hispanic population lives in states where Bank of America operates retail banks.

**Who was the first American-born Hispanic to be elected to the U.S. Senate?**

Dennis Chavez, who represented the state of New Mexico for 27 years. Chavez was born in Los Chavez (south of Albuquerque in Valencia County) in 1888. At age seven, his family moved to Albuquerque. When he was in the seventh grade, family circumstances forced him to quit school and begin paid employment. He eventually pursued his education, graduating from Georgetown University Law School. In 1920, when Chavez returned to Albuquerque to practice criminal law, he remained active in the Democratic party.

In 1934, Chavez ran against Republican U.S. Senator, Bronson Cutting, in a close, intense campaign. Chavez was defeated by a narrow margin and contested the election on the grounds of fraud. The issue was still pending when Cutting was killed in an airplane accident while returning to Washington. Governor Clyde Tingley appointed Chavez interim Senator and, in 1936, he was elected to complete the term. In the 1940s, Chavez proved to be a strong defender of civil rights. In 1944, he introduced a bill for the establishment of a Fair Employment Practices Commission "to prohibit discrimination in employment because of race, creed, national origin, or ancestry."[52]

**When did it become legal for women to vote in Albuquerque?**

On February 19, 1920, when New Mexico became the 32nd state to ratify the Suffrage Amendment.

**How was the County Sheriff position chosen before they were actually elected?**

In the 1880s, Perfecto Armijo and Santiago Baca took turns serving as 'peace officer.' To 'elect' a sheriff, these two would gather their toughest friends, meet in a vacant lot, and have a free-for-all battle with fists, sticks, and gun butts. A crowd gathered to watch and the man left standing with the most 'votes' from their 'supporters' won. Judge William Heacock was referee.[53]

**What was Judge Heacock's weakness?**

Judge William Heacock was a gambler, a card player, who often lost all of his money. When he did, he ordered a deputy to find him a drunk (one with money in his pockets) to charge with disorderly conduct. The Judge would hold a 'trial' and fine the man brought in the exact amount of money in his pockets.[54]

# The Business of Albuquerque

**What building in Old Town housed a bank, then a saloon, in quick succession?**

The Raynolds brothers' Central Bank, the first in Albuquerque, in Old Town (at the corners of South Plaza and Romero), relocated to New Albuquerque in 1881-82 and the building was quickly occupied for service as a saloon. The Central Bank was later absorbed by the First National Bank.[55]

**What was the biggest "industrial complex" in Albuquerque in 1875?**

Franz Huning's Molina de Glorieta flour mill, from its construction in 1860 to the arrival of the railroad in 1880. The mill burned in 1904. Within a year, Mr. Huning died.

**By 1900, what were the five most significant industries in Albuquerque?**

The most significant industry was the railroad. By 1900, the railroad employed 575 men, 60 engineers, and 60 firemen. The repair shops handled all of the work for the El Paso and Albuquerque to California lines of the Santa Fe.

The second largest industry was lumber. By 1905, the American Lumber Company was built on north Twelfth Street, and it rivaled the railroad as an employer. It produced milled lumber, doors, shingles, and other building materials in quantity for this region. The factory covered 110 acres,

Central Bank Building in Old Town, corner of James and Santiago, 1880. The Albuquerque Museum Photoarchives, PA1982.180.376.

employed 850 men and was one of the largest of this kind of business in the Southwest.

The third largest industry was established shortly after the railroad shop, and was a satellite business, the Albuquerque Foundry and Machine Works. It was built in 1881 to cast rolling stock for the railroads and to repair mining and manufacturing equipment. About 40 men were employed.

The Albuquerque Wool Scouring Mills and the allied Rio Grande Woolen Mills comprised the fourth major industry in Albuquerque. These firms accepted more than three million pounds of raw wool each year from New Mexico growers and either custom-scoured it for shipment to the East, or purchased it for the production of rugs, cloth, and clothing. About 40 persons were employed, many from nearby Martineztown.

The fifth largest industry in Albuquerque by 1900 was the Southwestern Brewery and Ice Company. This business was started in the 1880s to manufacture ice and beer for the local homes and saloons. By 1899, it proved so successful that the physical plant was enlarged and modernized, and shipments of beer were made to much of the Southwest. In 1900, 18 men were employed. The company produced 'Glorieta' and other brand beers for the saloons of Albuquerque.[56]

**Where were the first businesses in New Albuquerque located and what necessities and entertainment did they provide to the citizens of Albuquerque?**

The first businesses were located along Front Street (now First Street) facing the railroad tracks. They provided necessities, as well as entertainment. The businesses included saloons, restaurants, bakeries, hotels, dry good stores, lumber yards, and medical offices. The first business in New Albuquerque was reported to be a saloon comprised of a board over two kegs inside a tent where whiskey and beer cost five cents a shot. Businesses thrived here because of the central location of Albuquerque, and the railroad shipping facilities. Carloads of goods arrived daily from the East. These were stockpiled for wholesale and retail sale throughout New Mexico, southern Colorado, eastern Arizona, and west Texas.[57]

**Where was Albuquerque's "Wall Street" around the time of the turn of the century?**

The heart of Albuquerque's business district was situated along Railroad and Gold Avenues and up and down First and Second Streets. Gold Avenue was Albuquerque's "Wall Street." Most of Albuquerque's banks, real estate, and insurance offices were located along Gold. One could also find utility headquarters, the Commercial Club, newspapers, and other professional offices located there.[58]

**What department store was the first national chain store in Albuquerque?**

F.W. Woolworth Department Store was the first national chain store in Albuquerque. It was located at 317-319 W. Central Avenue about 1915. Nothing in the store cost more than fifteen cents.

Elias Stover and Co., Old Albuquerque Plaza, burro train, 1895. The Albuquerque Museum Photoarchives, PA1990.13.226.

**What is the signature New Mexico fast food chain?**

Blake's Lotaburger. By the end of 2005, there were 78 stores. Blake's Lotaburger was started by Blake Chanslor. The first Lotaburger restaurant opened on July 9, 1952 at Southern and San Mateo (in southeast Albuquerque) and is still there![59]

**Where was the first Albuquerque McDonald's located?**

The first McDonald's restaurant was opened in 1959 at 5900 Menaul NE. The original building was replaced in 1980. In 1959, hamburgers sold for fifteen cents and cheeseburgers were nineteen cents.

**When was Albuquerque designated as a major national center for military research?**

During World War II. The population grew by more than ten times in the next five decades. The data shown below demonstrates Albuquerque's dramatic population increases.[60]

| | |
|---|---|
| 1940 | 35,449 |
| 1950 | 96,815 |
| 1960 | 201,189 |
| 1970 | 244,501 |
| 1980 | 332,336 |

In the most recent years, the rapid population increase in Albuquerque continues:[61]

| | |
|---|---|
| 1990 | 386,988 |
| 2000 | 448,607 |
| 2005 | 484,246 |

**What were the precursors to modern hospitals in Albuquerque?**

Between 1902 and 1915, several sanitoriums were constructed in Albuquerque, intended for the treatment of tuberculosis. Two became modern hospitals: St. Joseph and Presbyterian.

**How many major medical hospitals does Albuquerque have?**

Nine. They are: New Mexico Veterans Affairs Health Care System, Presbyterian Hospital, University of New Mexico Hospital, Heart Hospital of New Mexico, Kaseman Presbyterian Hospital, Lovelace Medical Center, Lovelace West Mesa Medical Center, Albuquerque Regional Medical Center, and the Women's Hospital.

**How did Lovelace Medical Center gain international recognition?**

It was the testing site for the original Mercury astronauts.

**What does Albuquerque provide to the state of New Mexico?**

It is the state's center for finance, communications, transportation, medical facilities, research and development, and cultural amenities.

**Where was the first J.C. Penney's store in Albuquerque?**

In 1916, it was located at 410 W. Central. It was the oldest continually operated chain store in Albuquerque.[62]

**What business was originally on the site that is now Kelly's Brew Pub, an historic landmark in Albuquerque?**

The Jones Motor Company, built in 1939, which was a gas station, car dealership, and repair shop that served motorists along Route 66, as well as the early suburbs on the East Mesa. The Jones Motor Company moved to a new location in 1957 and other businesses occupied this building until it was officially designated an historic building in 1993. Kelly's has renovated and restored many original design elements.[63]

# Sports in Albuquerque

**What sports were popular in Albuquerque around the turn of the century?**

Sports such as baseball and bicycling were popular. Photographs of that period indicate that bicycling clubs were well established from 1885-1910.

**What was the name of Albuquerque's baseball team in 1894?**

The Albuquerque Browns. The team was named after the St. Louis Browns by W.T. McCreight, then city editor of the *Daily Citizen.* The Browns were winners of the 1894 New Mexico tournament with McCreight as their manager.[64]

**What important event occurred at the territorial fair in 1909 and launched a sport that made Albuquerque popular worldwide?**

In 1909, Joseph Blondin and Roy Stamm made the first successful long distance balloon flight during the fair.

**What are the dates of the first manned balloon flights in Albuquerque?**

On July 4, 1882, a bartender by the name of 'Professor' Park A. Van Tassel acquired a gas bag and basket from California and made a free ascension from Second Street between Railroad and Gold Avenues. The bag was filled from the city gas plant. Van Tassel reached an altitude of 14,207 feet and landed in a cornfield near Old Town.

The next balloon flight took place during the Territorial Fair of 1909. Joseph Blondin was a musician turned aeronaut and he convinced fair officials that they needed a balloon in which captive rides could be given followed by a free ascension.[65]

**Where is the nearest ski area?**

Minutes away from Albuquerque is the Sandia Peak Ski Area, with twin base-to-summit chair lifts to its upper slopes at 10,378 feet and a 1,700 foot vertical drop. There are twenty-two trails, a family area, and fourteen trails for intermediates.

**Who is called the 'father of skiing' in Albuquerque?**

Bob Nordhaus, who grew up in Albuquerque, but later lived in the east where he spent time skiing. In 1936 he organized the Albuquerque Ski Club. There was no ski area at the time. Nordhaus and his wife skied by walking up slopes and sliding down. That same year, the U.S. Forest Service cleared land for a slope at Tree Spring in the Sandias and established a system of trails. This became the La Madera Ski Area.

The Balloon Ascension of Park Van Tassel, owner of the Elite Saloon on Railroad Ave., photograph taken on Second St. between Railroad Ave. and Gold Ave., 1882. The Albuquerque Museum Photoarchives, PA1978.50.36.

When Nordhaus returned after the war in 1945, he started a rope tow at La Madera. Lift tickets were $1. In 1957, Ben Abruzzo became ski area manager and bought half the assets from Nordhaus. Two years later the road to the ski area was paved. In 1963, the name of the ski area was changed to Sandia Peak; a double chair lift and a mountain top restaurant were added.[66]

**What year was professional baseball born in Albuquerque?**

Professional baseball was born in Albuquerque in 1931. The team name was the Albuquerque Dons and later the Albuquerque Cardinals. In the late 1940s and early 1950s, owners and organizers were trying anything to keep generating support for a bunch of guys who just wanted to play ball.

**Who were the Albuquerque Dukes?**

The community-owned Dukes played for the West Texas-New Mexico Class B baseball league in 1955.

In 1956, admission was 75 cents, Coke was a dime, and a seat cushion was fifteen cents.

In 1956, Albuquerque was promoted to the Class A Western League. With that improvement came a front-office guru named Purk Purnage.

There was a time when the team was being kept alive by a handful of true baseball fans in the community. The "Save the Dukes" drive was an annual event.

In 1958, the team wasn't enough to keep the fledgling Western League alive. The league folded in 1958 and for the first time since 1945, there was no professional baseball in Albuquerque.

The Albuquerque Dodgers became a part of the Los Angeles Dodger organization in 1963, playing AA baseball until 1971. In 1972, the Dodgers moved their Spokane AAA ball club to Albuquerque to become the Dukes and began using the "Duke head" logo. In April of 1969, professional baseball was first played in the Sports Stadium.

The Albuquerque Dukes of the AAA Pacific Coast League was the number one farm team of the Los Angeles Dodgers. They played 72 baseball games from April to September in the city-owned Albuquerque Sports Stadium.

The Albuquerque Dukes played their final regular season home game at the Sports Stadium on August 22, 2000. Albuquerque's franchise in the Triple-A Pacific Coast League was sold to a group from Portland, Oregon. The team moved to the Pacific Northwest for the next season. 11,424 fans showed up to watch the regular-season finale that was followed by fireworks. Dukes' general manager Pat McKernan fought back tears as he threw out the first pitch.[67]

**Who are the Albuquerque Isotopes?**

On April 11, 2003, the Albuquerque Isotopes played the first professional baseball game in the Duke City since the Albuquerque Dukes left following their 2000 season. 12,215 fans showed up on Opening Day at Isotopes Park. That season ended with the Isotopes winning the Central Division Title and earning a berth in the Pacific Coast League Playoffs.[68]

**What Albuquerque native and graduate of Eldorado High School (where he was a four year letterman in four sports) went on to be the starting quarterback for the Los Angeles Rams football team?**

Jim Everett. He retired in 1998 after twelve seasons as one of the NFL's most reliable quarterbacks.

**What is the name of the team that once played professional hockey at Tingley Coliseum?**

The New Mexico Scorpions of the Central Hockey League. Their new home is at the Santa Ana Star Center in Rio Rancho.

**What are the colors sported by the University of New Mexico Lobos?**

Cherry and silver. These colors are symbols, according to the 1897 *Mirage*, of a Sandia sunset and the silver ribbon of the Rio Grande. In 1973, turquoise was added to the basketball uniforms, but was never officially accepted by the UNM regents to represent the university.

**Who is Albuquerque's most recent Olympic medalist?**

Trent Dimas. At 21, in Barcelona, he was the 1992 gold medalist in the men's high bar competition with a score of 9.875. Even when the Spanish announcer called him "Dimas Trent," he smiled.

**Who were Albuquerque's first Olympic medalists?**

In 1972, two New Mexicans came home with Olympic medals (three of thirty-three captured by U.S. athletes). Cathy Carr, a 19-year old Albuquerque swimmer set a world record in the 100-meter breast stroke at 1:13.58. She was a member of the 400-meter medley relay team that posted another world record: 4:20.85. Albuquerquean, 18-year old Janet Ely, qualified first in ten meter diving and third off the three meter board.

**How many public golf courses does Albuquerque boast?**

There are seven: Arroyo Del Oso Golf Course, Desert Greens Golf Course, Ladera Golf Course, Los Altos Golf Course, Puerto del Sol Golf Course, University of New Mexico Golf Course (North), and University of New Mexico Golf Course (South).

**Who is the greatest boxer Albuquerque ever produced?**

Bob Foster, whose career consisted of 65 fights over 17 years. Foster became world Light Heavyweight Champion in 1968 and successfully defended his title 14 times. When the world Heavyweight Title was his goal, he took on Joe Frazier and Muhammad Ali. The only losses on his record are to heavyweights. As a light heavy, Foster was undefeated. He retired in 1974, returned to the ring for seven fights, then retired for good in 1978. Foster lives here in Albuquerque.

**Who are the recent world champion boxers from Albuquerque?**

Johnny "Mi Vida Loca" Tapia is a five-time world champion. In 1995 he won the WBO World Junior Bantamweight championship. In 1998 he went up in weight and won the WBA World Bantamweight title. Tapia lost that title belt to Paulie Ayala in 1999, but soon after won the WBO world title belt. In 2002, Tapia won the IBF World Featherweight champion, becoming one of a small group of boxers to win world titles in three different divisions. He lost that title but won it back in 2003. His nickname is a reflection of his past. He once had a heated rivalry with Danny Romero, who is a three-time world champion. Romero's father trained them both and Tapia's split from them was not on good terms.[69]

Danny "Kid Dynamite" Romero won the title of the IBF's World Flyweight champion in 1995; in 1996, he had moved up to the Super Flyweight division and won his second world title. In July of 1997, Romero and Tapia met in a much hyped fight in Las Vegas, Nevada. Tapia won in a twelve round unanimous decision. Romero retired in May, 2003, after a win that gave him the IBA's Super-Bantamweight title.[70]

**Who is Notah Begay III?**

Begay, from Albuquerque, is the first Native American player to reach top-ten status on the PGA. He also was the only player who could putt equally well right-handed or left-handed.[71]

**Who was Coach Roy Johnson?**

Johnson came to UNM in 1920 and oversaw the construction of Carlisle Gym, as well as the first grass football field with bleachers. The UNM Athletic Department then became competitive among colleges in the Western United States. Johnson also oversaw construction of Johnson Center on the UNM campus, which opened in 1957. Johnson coached until 1959. The Lobos won 157 games with Johnson as head basketball coach.[72]

**Which Lobo Basketball coach was responsible for the building of "The Pit" in Albuquerque in 1966?**

Bob King, also known as the "Architect of Lobo Basketball." When he began at the University of New Mexico, games were held at the 7,000 seat Johnson Gym. King was responsible for doubling UNM's attendance in his first three years, causing school officials to realize that a bigger place to play was needed. The Pit (University Arena) seats 18,000. In 1992, UNM President, Richard Peck, announced that the court at the University Arena would be named in honor of Bob King. In 1999, The Pit was recognized by Sports Illustrated as one of the top-20 sporting venues of the 20$^{th}$ century.[73]

**Who is the legendary coach, known as "Papa Dog" to Albuquerque High School?**

Jim Hulsman, who coached for 41 years at AHS, 34 as head basketball coach. Today Hulsman is on the faculty at the University of New Mexico, teaching Basketball Theory. In his den at home, he has a closet filled with binders containing years of Bulldog memories, which is really the school's history.

Hulsman compiled a record of 660 victories and 223 losses. Under his direction, Albuquerque High teams won seven state championships (1971, 1977, 1984, 1990, 1993, 1995 and 1998). Hulsman took the school to 24 New Mexico state tournaments. In 1990, he was inducted into the Albuquerque Sports Hall of Fame. Coach Hulsman was also inducted into the New Mexico High School Coaches Association Hall of Honor in 1997, and, in 1999, the New Mexico Activities Association Hall of Pride and Honor. In 2002, he was named National Coach of the Year by both the National Federation Coaches Association and the National High School Athletic Coaches Association. In 1999, Hulsman was inducted into the National Hall of Fame by the National High School Athletic Coaches Association and into the National Federation of State High School Associations Hall of Fame in 2003.

In 2003, the UNM Alumni Association Board of Directors honored Jim Hulsman with the Bernard S. Rodey Award. This award is given to someone who has devoted an unusual amount of time in a leadership capacity and has contributed significantly to the field of education.

A native of Pittsburgh, Pennsylvania, Hulsman came to New Mexico in 1940 and graduated from Albuquerque High School in 1949, where he lettered in football.

**Who is the Sacramento Kings forward who began his career as a Lobo basketball player?**

Kenny Thomas, who played as a senior at Albuquerque High School. He attended the University of New Mexico, where he is second on the all-time scoring list, career blocks list, and career dunks list. He leads the school's lists in career rebounds, freshman scoring and rebounding, and personal fouls for a season and career.

Thomas was one of five Lobos to be selected as an All-American in 1998. He was selected by the Houston Rockets as the 22nd pick in the 1999 NBA Draft. He was traded to Philadelphia during the 2002-03 season. In 2005, Kenny Thomas was traded to the Sacramento Kings.[74]

**Who is the female boxer from Albuquerque that continues to move up in national prominence?**

Holly Holm, a preacher's daughter, who was rated by insidewomensboxing.com as the third best pound-for-pound fighter in the women's ranks as of September, 2006. Holm (14-1, 5 KOs) was ranked behind Laila Ali (22-0, 19 KOs) and Ann Wolfe (24-1, 16 KOs). Holms is the IBA junior welter and WBA welterweight champ. [75]

Holly Holms graduated from Manzano High School in 2000. Her career in boxing began with aerobics and kickboxing. She was instructed in both by Mike Winklejohn, who is now her trainer. Winklejohn said in late 2005 that his goal was to get Holm recognized on the national level. He also expressed interest in getting her to Las Vegas, saying "And I don't see anything wrong with taking advantage of her looks. Michael Jordan did it...Holly is a cute girl."[76] That she is.

**Who is the female Duke city native that placed fourth in the 2004 Olympics in the heptathlon?**

Sheila Burrell. The heptathlon is a grueling competition that consists of seven events: 200 meter and 800 meter runs, 100 meter hurdles, shot put, javelin throw, high jump and long jump. Sheila qualified for the U.S. team in the 2000 Olympics, but a knee injury kept her from finishing in the top.

Burrell won state titles as a senior in high school in the 200 and 400 meter dashes, the long jump and the high jump. She was also a standout in other sports and had college scholarship offers in track, basketball and volleyball. She accepted the one from UCLA in track and field. The Albuquerque Sports Hall of Fame has honored Burrell with its Award of Distinction three times: in 2001, 2003 and 2004.[77]

**What Sandia High School graduate is now a Major League Baseball relief pitcher with the Los Angeles Angels of Anaheim?**

Brendan Donnelly, who was drafted in 1992 by the Chicago White Sox. He spent ten seasons with them before making his debut in major league baseball.

**Who is the heir apparent to former Lobos great Brian Urlacher?**

Nick Speegle, who graduated from La Cueva High School in 2000. At La Cueva, he was first-team all-state defensive end and second-team all-state tight end, while earning a 4.32 cumulative GPA taking honors classes.

He had a spectacular career while playing for the UNM Lobos football team; he earned All-Mountain West Conference honorable mention in 2002. He graduated from the University in 2004 with a degree in general management and a 3.97 cumulative GPA. He was pursuing his Masters in Sport Administration when he was drafted to the Cleveland Browns. In 2006, he was traded to the San Diego Chargers.

**Who is Albuquerque's Ultimate Fighting Champion?**

25-year old Diego "Nightmare" Sanchez. Sanchez is a mixed martial artist with a background in wrestling and Gaidojutsu, a system of submission wrestling. As a senior at Del Norte High School, he won the state wrestling championship in the 152-pound weight class. He won a contract with the Ultimate Fighting Championship after winning the first season of their reality show, *The Ultimate Fighter*, in 2005.[78]

The Ultimate Fighting Championship is a U.S.-based mixed martial arts (MMA) organization. It is now the major MMA promotion in North America. The UFC began as a tournament to find the world's best fighter, no matter their style. It was initially known as 'no holds barred' fighting and it allowed fighters of various disciplines to prove which martial arts style prevailed above others. Before the UFC reformed itself, it was forced underground and banned from the Pay-Per-View programming because of accusations of brutality that was more spectacle than sport. The UFC now has emerged as a legitimate sporting event and become sanctioned by athletic commissions. The UFC has become popular again with its cable TV deal with Fox Sports Net and Spike TV. A contract with the UFC for the winner of *The Ultimate Fighter* title provides three fights and a six-figure salary.

**What two Albuquerque high school graduates played for the UNM football team then went on to the NFL?**

Jarrod Baxter, Running Back for the Arizona Cardinals was drafted in 2002 by the Houston Texans.

Baxter was a 1997 graduate of Highland High School and was a four-year starter for the Lobos. Baxter received the L.F. "Tow" Diehm Inspirational Award from UNM for the 2001-02 season.

Ryan Cook, a 2001 graduate of Cibola High School, was the first center in UNM history named first team All-Mountain West Conference three times. He was drafted in 2006 to the Minnesota Vikings.

**Who was "Tow" Diehm?**

"Tow" Diehm was known as the "father of Athletic Training" in the State of New Mexico. He became the Head Athletic Trainer at the University of New Mexico in 1957 and remained in that position until 1988. He established one of the first educational programs in Athletic Training in the United States. He promoted the hiring of athletic trainers in Albuquerque High Schools and around the state of New Mexico. He lobbied for and secured passage of one of the first licensure laws governing athletic training in the United States. He was one of the founders of the New Mexico Athletic Trainers' Association.

Among the many, many honors and awards received by Diehm are those from the Albuquerque Sports Hall of Fame, the National Athletic Trainers' Association Hall of Fame, the Rocky Mountain Athletic Trainers' Association Hall of Fame, and the New Mexico Athletic Trainers' Association Hall of Fame. UNM honored his memory by naming the athletic facility at University Stadium after him.[79] This state of the art facility is one of the finest in the country. The facility is open to all UNM student athletes and they train in the All Sport Weight Room, which was funded by a $547,000 donation from Pepsi-Cola West.

**Which two Albuquerque natives were teammates on the UNM Lobo Men's Soccer Team when it became NCAA Runner-Up in 2005 and also went on to play Major League Soccer?**

Brandon Moss (Eldorado High School) and Jeff Rowland (La Cueva High School). These two are among 7 former Lobos in the Pros. Moss plays for the Columbus Crew and Rowland for the Real Salt Lake.

**When did the Lobos win the NCAA Skiing Championships?**

In 2004, the University of New Mexico Ski Team brought home the first ever NCAA team title to the University. The Lobos finished 42 points ahead of Utah, the defending national champion.

**Who has become the 'winningest' coach in New Mexico women's basketball history, giving the Lady Lobos national recognition?**

Under Don Flanagan, the UNM women's basketball team has finished in the upper half of the Mountain West Conference for six straight years. Flanagan has coached the UNM team for eleven years, and the fan support has grown every year. In 2005, New Mexico finished fourth in the nation in average attendance for the fourth straight season. The Lady Lobos have had three appearances in the NCAA Tournament.

Before UNM, Flanagan coached girl's basketball at Eldorado High School for sixteen years. He led that team to numerous records, including 14 tournament championships,

15 district championships, and 11 state championships. He coached the girls for nine undefeated seasons and Eldorado High was named the Albuquerque Sports Hall of Fame Team of the Year in 1987.

Among his many honors, the Albuquerque Journal and the Albuquerque Tribune have each named Flanagan Coach of the Year six times. He was inducted into the Albuquerque Sports Hall of Fame for Lifetime Achievement in 1997.

# Albuquerque Utilities and Transportation

**What was the first public transportation in Albuquerque?**

The first public transportation was the Albuquerque Street Railroad, a horsedrawn line. It operated from 1881 to 1904 and its route was between Old Town and New Albuquerque using Railroad Avenue. Oliver Cromwell, a New York investor, bought the business and paid for its construction. Electric trolleys replaced the horsedrawn cars and operated from 1904 to 1927.

**By what year did Albuquerque develop far enough to have services found in most eastern cities?**

Utilities and services developed rapidly. Developers submitted proposals to the county, prior to 1885, for exclusive rights to build electric, gas, water and telephone franchises, which were granted for specified periods of time. By 1885, one could have had all the desired services found in most eastern cities.

**When were telephones first used in Albuquerque?**

A telephone system was begun in Albuquerque by Miguel Otero, Sr. in 1882. It started in an adobe building in the 100 block of Railroad Avenue with 50 subscribers. There was no long distance service and it was not popular immediately. In 1887, the Colorado Telephone System bought out Otero, but despite improvements, subscribers dwindled. A competing Mutual Automatic Telephone Company was organized in 1901, featuring dial phones.

**In what year was the first long distance telephone line installed in Albuquerque?**

The first long distance line was installed in 1911. Prior to that, in 1906, the Colorado Telephone System bought out the Mutual Automatic Company. Dial phones vanished from Albuquerque until the 1940s.

**Before the bridge was built, spanning the width of the Rio Grande River, how did people get across when necessary?**

When the (Rio Grande) river was low, the rural folk on their way to market or church in Albuquerque just rolled up their trousers or skirts and waded across. At other times, they used log canoes or skiffs, which they propelled with long poles.

**When did Albuquerque get its first ferry boat?**

About 1856, Albuquerque got its first ferry boat. It was provided by Major James Carleton, acting-commander of the military post. The new ferry was launched at a convenient crossing near the present Barelas Bridge. Although it remained under government ownership, operation was delegated to local workers who were paid by the month.

Around the docking site on the east bank, a small community called Placers grew up. It was later washed away by one of the Rio Grande's spring floods.

Mountain States Telephone Co., operators on long distance switchboards, 1953. The Albuquerque Museum Photoarchives, PA1980.187.521.

**Why is the name "Double Eagle II" significant to Albuquerque?**

In 1978, three self-made businessmen from Albuquerque made the first flight across the Atlantic Ocean by men in a balloon. Maxie Anderson, Ben Abruzzo, and Larry Newman made the five day, seventeen hour flight in a balloon named "Double Eagle II," successor to "Double Eagle," the balloon in which Anderson and Abruzzo attempted this same flight and failed in 1977.

The flight began near Presque Isle, Maine, and ended when the balloon landed in a barley field near the village of Misery, France. The success did not come about merely from the completion of the flight on August 17, 1978, but also, from the fact that it was a courageous, second attempt by these adventurous individuals who met their challenge head on.

The Double Eagle II Airport was dedicated by Mayor Harry Kinney on October 5, 1983. It was named in honor of the Double Eagle II balloon. The actual balloon and gondola now reside at the Smithsonian Air and Space Museum in Washington D.C.[80]

Maxie Anderson died in a balloon accident in Germany in 1983. Ben Abruzzo, along with his wife, Pat, died in an airplane accident in Albuquerque in 1985. Larry Newman miraculously survived a skydiving accident in 1995. After a year of recovery, he returned to his job as a pilot for America West Airlines.

**In what year was the first airplane flight made in New Mexico?**

In 1911, a plane took off from the territorial fair grounds in Albuquerque. Pilot Charles F. Walsh lifted his

Curtiss biplane from the infield track of the fairgrounds to Old Town on October 11. He made a flight of 27 miles from Old Town to the Barelas Bridge, then back for a landing on the fair track. He covered this distance in ten minutes.[81]

**How many national airlines serve Albuquerque and surrounding areas?**

Eight major commercial carriers. They are: American Airlines, America West Airlines, Continental Airlines, Delta Air Lines, Frontier Airlines, Northwest Airlines, Southwest Airlines, and United Airlines. Regional service is provided to Albuquerque by Shuttle America, Horizon Air, Mesa Airlines, and Skywest Airlines. Albuquerque also receives regular service from two commuter airlines: Mesa Airlines and Great Lakes Airlines.

**When was Albuquerque's first airport built?**

In 1928, two Santa Fe Railroad employees, Frank Speakman and William Franklin, built runways on leased acreage, creating an air field on the East Mesa. The new facility was named Albuquerque Airport, even though it was a private venture. Entrepreneur James Oxnard, a New York air transportation promoter, bought out Franklin's interest in the Albuquerque Airport and established a new company to operate the local venture. It was Oxnard who was responsible for the addition of new hangars, lights, beacons, and expanded runways. By 1929, Albuquerque's airfield had attracted two competing carriers – Western Air Express and Trans-Continental Air Transport. Western Air moved to the West Mesa in 1929, becoming Albuquerque's second airfield. The two airlines merged in 1930 and became TWA

(Transcontinental and Western Air). The West Mesa airport then acquired the name of Albuquerque Airport and the East Mesa airfield was known as Oxnard Field.

Before the two airlines merged, Transcontinental Air Transport began construction of its administration building that included a Fred Harvey dining room. The first all-electric “Harvey House” restaurant was decorated in Southwestern style, with vigas, Indian rugs, and art.[82]

In 1935, TWA suggested that Albuquerque have a municipal airport. In 1939, the municipal airport opened with one of the longest runways in the country. Albuquerque Municipal Airport was constructed three miles west of Oxnard Field and near the present International Airport complex.

During the two decades following its completion, the people of Albuquerque came to the airport just to watch the planes take off, to just sit at the Fred Harvey Café located inside the airport and watch the people, or to mail a letter. Everyone said that when a letter was mailed from the airport, it arrived faster.

Albuquerque International Sunport terminal opened in 1965. It was designed to handle traffic for 25 years. Another addition became necessary in 1973 because of the faster than anticipated growth of air travel. The terminal was expanded in the late 1980s and again in 1996, to its present size. It was long referred to as the Sunport, but became Albuquerque International when customs clearance offices were established here.

TWA plane outside Albuquerque Airport, 1949. Photographer Clarence Redman. The Albuquerque Museum Photoarchives, PA1980.185.480.

The old Airport Terminal, at 2920 Yale SE, is an historic landmark in Albuquerque. The old Terminal opened in 1939 and served Albuquerque until 1965, when a new terminal was constructed. The Works Progress Administration funded the construction of the terminal building, which included rich Southwestern detail. During World War II, the U.S. Government operated out of the terminal. This led to the establishment of the Albuquerque Army Air Field, and eventually Kirtland Air Force Base. The Old Terminal was placed on the National Register of Historic Places in 1989.[83]

**In the 1890s, what was Albuquerque known as "first in New Mexico" for?**

It was the first New Mexico city to use electric lights.[84]

**Who was A.W. Whipple?**

He established the first road from Albuquerque to California.[85]

**What year did the famous Route 66 begin to be traveled and when did it cease to be?**

U.S. Highway 66 was commissioned in 1923. By the year 1927, it was fully paved from Chicago to Los Angeles. Route 66 was decommissioned in 1985 with completion of the National Interstate Highway system. Interstate Highways (I-25 and I-40) now are numbered with even numbers to designate east/west travel and odd numbers to designate north/south travel.

# Naming Folklore of Albuquerque

**Where did the city get its name?**

According to author and historian, Marc Simmons, the city took its name from the Duke of Alburquerque, Viceroy of New Spain, who spelled that name with an extra 'r.' Spanish and Mexican documents continued to use the traditional spelling into the 1840s. Simmons claims that it was the coming to New Mexico of the Anglo-Americans that led to the change in spelling.

**How were settlements named?**

When new families joined existing ones on communal land grants or abutting land, they honored the village's founder by adopting his or her family name for their cluster of houses.[86]

**What were the first residential districts to be developed in Albuquerque?**

The first residential districts to be developed were Franz Huning's Highland Addition (1880), between Copper and Iron Avenues and High Street and the railroad tracks, and the Perea Addition (1881) in what now is called the Downtown Neighborhood District from Eleventh through Fifteenth Streets between Central and Lomas Avenues.

**What name did Central Avenue used to have?**

Railroad Avenue until 1912, when it became Central Avenue. Beginning in 1937, Route 66 crossed Albuquerque along Central Avenue.

**What are several streets in Albuquerque named for?**

Several streets in Albuquerque were given the names of early Hispanic plazas, chapels, and extended family settlements. Some of these are Barelas, Atrisco, and Ranchos de Albuquerque.

**What did the name of Rio Grande Boulevard used to be?**

Main Street in 1876 is now Rio Grande Boulevard.

**Why was the name "Sandia" Mountains chosen?**

Sandia, in Spanish, means watermelon. The name was chosen because of the resemblance of the mountain range to a slice of watermelon. At sunset, there is a red coloration across the top of the mountain because of the effect of the sun's rays on the granite exposed on the western face. Near the ridge line at the summit, the green rind of the watermelon is seen in the Pennsylvania limestone and a cover of dark timber.[87]

**What is the name of the famous car racing family who lives in Albuquerque?**

Unser. The Unser family has resided in Albuquerque since 1936. Bobby Unser, Sr. won the Indy 500 in 1968, 1975, and again in 1981. Al Unser, Sr. won Indy in 1970, 1971, 1978, and 1987. Al Unser, Jr. was the winner of the Indy 500 in 1991 and 1994. Shortly after Bobby won the Indy for the third time in 1981, 84th Street was renamed Unser Boulevard to honor this family who has won more Indy 500s than any other family.

It is said that when Al Unser, Sr. started racing, there was only one driver he wanted to beat: his brother, Bobby. Al is the youngest of four racing brothers.

**What were "hornos" used for?**

In open courtyards, Albuquerque's colonial settlers baked bread in hornos, domed adobe ovens.

**What is meant by the "bosque"?**

The "bosque" refers to a belt of Cottonwood trees that spreads a canopy of shade along the river banks of the Rio Grande. These groves are the most attractive feature of the lowlands. Cottonwoods grow rapidly and, in summer, their green foliage spreads welcome shade upon the river banks. In autumn, the foliage becomes a blaze of gold.

These trees are large; some reach 100 feet tall with trunks four feet in diameter. Starting in the north and moving south, the Bosque winds its way through the cities of Bernalillo, Sandia Pueblo, Corrales, Alameda, Albuquerque, then through the communities of Atrisco, Armijo, Pajarito, and Los Padillas.

## How does Albuquerque remember John Baker?

John Willard Baker grew up in Albuquerque during the 1950s and early 1960s. He was a star athlete at Manzano High School. In his junior year, he won recognition by defeating the reigning cross-country champion. He continued his education at the University of New Mexico, where he led the school team to a series of brilliant victories. He was victorious over some of the nation's best track teams. By 1968, he was ranked eighth on the world indoor list of milers. Upon receiving his degree, he accepted a position as coach at Albuquerque's Aspen Elementary School.

On May 26, 1969, while jogging, he collapsed. After driving himself to a hospital, medical tests revealed he had cancer throughout his body. The doctors gave him only six months to live. He did not stay in the hospital, but carried on his coaching duties at Aspen Elementary and also helped coach the "Duke City Dashers" (an Albuquerque all girl youth track club). He died at age 26 on Thanksgiving day, 1970.

In May, 1971, at the request of the students, Aspen Elementary changed its name to become John Baker Elementary School. In August of 1975, BYU produced a 30 minute video highlighting John's career and stressing his courage. The video was used throughout the United States as an inspiration for "Youth at Risk."

*The Readers Digest* ran a feature story on John which was followed by a book by William J. Buchanan, entitled *A Shining Season.* A made-for-TV movie by the same name was produced in 1979.

In April of 1980, he was inducted into the Albuquerque Sports Hall of Fame and in 1991 became a member of the prestigious University of New Mexico Alumni Athlete Hall of Honor.

**What is “The Pit”?**

The arena where the University of New Mexico Lobos play basketball. It has been dubbed “The Pit” because the playing floor and seating are situated below ground level.

**Who is Greg MacAleese?**

An ex-Albuquerque policeman (also an ex-Canadian) who, in 1976, began the CrimeStoppers program in Albuquerque. Greg became a U.S. citizen in order to become a police officer. He was a detective investigating the murder of a young University of New Mexico student in 1976 when he had the idea of asking a local TV station if the crime could be enacted during a newscast to possibly get an eyewitness to the crime to come forward. It worked. After that, local businesses and citizens volunteered their time and money to create the Albuquerque Metro Crime Stoppers.

Crime Stoppers is now worldwide, with 1,100 programs.

**What is the name of the first national environmental advocacy and watchdog organization in Albuquerque?**

The Sierra Club. This organization, founded in 1892, is America’s most effective advocate for the environment. It helps to protect the environment both locally and globally. There are now over 750,000 members in the U.S. Members get involved with community issues as well as lobbying on a national level. Involvement helps to preserve wilderness and wildlife, which are irreplaceable. The Rio Grande Chapter, which encompasses all of New Mexico and El Paso, Texas, was begun in 1963. There is an office of the Rio Grande Chapter at 110 2nd St. SW.

### Who was Dr. Elijio Osuna?

A physician that came to Albuquerque in the 1890s from Monterrey, Mexico. He delivered many babies in Albuquerque. He was a coroner as well. His daughter, Anita Osuna y Martinez de Carr, was the first Hispanic woman on the UNM faculty. Osuna Road was named for the good doctor in 1945.[88]

### Who was Coors Road named for?

Henry G. Coors, a district attorney and judge in Albuquerque in the 1940s and early 1950s.[89]

### What are land grants?

In order to promote settlement on the frontier, the Spanish king gave land to individuals, groups, and towns through a system of land grants, or *Mercedes*. Spanish authorities used this system in other states like California or Florida, but the New Mexico land grants are the oldest. There were two kinds of land grants: individual and community. The individual grant required that the individual live on the land and improve it for years before receiving title. The community land grant was given to settlers who wanted to establish a new town.

Land grants were also given to reward patrons of the Spanish government and military officers.

Spain issued land grants to several Indian Pueblo groups who had occupied the areas long before Spanish settlers arrived. In Albuquerque, the Spanish governor awarded grants to the Sandia and Isleta Pueblos.

Community land grants were organized around a central plaza, with each household receiving an allotment and a tract of land to farm.

In The Treaty of Hidalgo in 1848, the U.S. agreed to recognize land grants made by the Spanish and Mexican government in New Mexico and five other states.[90]

## What is unique about the Atrisco land grant?

Settlers were farming and raising livestock at Atrisco, which is on the western bank of the Rio Grande, long before "La Villa de Alburquerque" existed. The government of Spain granted 41,533 acres to Don Fernando Duran y Chávez. The grant was payment for his father's services in the Reconquest after the Pueblo Revolt. In 1703, the provincial government recognized Atrisco as a town.

In 1892, the Town of Atrisco became a community land grant corporation. In 1967, the Legislature allowed the Atrisco Land Grant to form a private corporation, Westland Development Co. Heirs of the original settlers received shares in the company and shares can only be transferred to other heirs.

Not only is Atrisco one of the oldest existing land grants in the United States, but it is one of the only Spanish Colonial grants still presently owned by the heirs of its original settlers.[91]

## What area is known as Martineztown?

Martineztown is actually three neighborhoods: North Martineztown, South Martineztown and Santa Barbara. Martineztown began when families in the 1800s drove their herds east to the sandhills for summer grazing and camped there. Martineztown had a large acequia (crude watering hole/ditch). Around 1850, Don Manuel Martin moved his family permanently to this area, which became known as Los Martines, and later, Martineztown. Don Martin's descendants still live in this area. The first church in Martineztown was built by the Presbyterians in 1889. The church that replaced the smaller one still stands at the northeast corner of Edith and Lomas Boulevards. In 1916, San Ignacio Catholic Church was built on Edith Boulevard between Mountain Road and Indian School. Martineztown's boundaries are Broadway, I-25, Martin Luther King Blvd. and Mountain Road.

**What was the original name of Roosevelt Park?**

Terrace Park. The park was completed in 1935 during the middle of the Great Depression. Albuquerque's mayor at the time, Clyde Tingley, was close friends with President Franklin Roosevelt. The park was built with federal Civil Works Administration funding. Soon after its opening, the park's name was changed to Roosevelt Park. An historic landmark in Albuquerque, the cost was $122,338 to transform the 13 acres into a beautiful, lush park, which remains virtually unchanged after 70 years.[92]

**What two intersecting streets in Old Town once had names that meant the same in English as well as Spanish?**

James Street and Santiago Street intersected southwest of Old Town Plaza in the 1880s and 1890s. Today, Santiago Street is Romero Street and James Street has become South Plaza Street.

**What is the distinguished ancestry of Erna Fergusson?**

Erna Fergusson, noted journalist, author and lecturer, was born in 1888 to Clara Mary Huning and Harvey Butler Fergusson. Her mother was the daughter of Franz and Ernestine Huning. Her father was a delegate to Congress, elected from New Mexico from 1897 to 1899, and again, from 1912 until 1915. He was successful in obtaining the passage of the Fergusson Act in 1898, a statute which granted to New Mexico four million acres of public domain in trust for the use and benefit in perpetuity of the common schools of New Mexico.[93]

# Education in Albuquerque

**In 1891, when a group of philanthropic women called a meeting to discuss creation of a community library, what did they come up with?**

The Albuquerque Public Library was founded in 1891. More than $1,000 was pledged at that meeting and a room was reserved in the Commercial Club to house the collection. The city later assumed the library and paid for part of its operation through taxes. Private association fund-raisers continued to be necessary.[94]

**What creation was said to be "the brightest jewel in Albuquerque's crown" in 1889?**

The University of New Mexico, also known as UNM. Bernard S. Rodey, a local lawyer, drew up the legislation creating the institution in 1889. In 1892, the first building, Hodgin Hall, was completed. Courses consisted of four-year programs in Latin-Scientific, English and Normal work and a one-year commercial course.

**Who was responsible for opening the first public school building in Albuquerque?**

"Public education in Albuquerque began under the impetus of religious organization. In 1877, Jesuits at San Felipe de Neri in Old Town opened the first public school building (still standing) just northwest of the church.

Hodgin Hall, lone building on the East Mesa, Sandia Mountains in background, 1902. The Albuquerque Museum Photoarchives, PA1978.50.716.

In 1881, the sisters of Charity, among them Sister Blandina, assumed responsibility for the school, which was partially subsidized by the county.

In 1879, a public school system was created, and an Academy, sponsored by the Protestant Colorado College of Colorado Springs, founded a nondenominational school on the plaza. By 1890, the Academy had built a new structure, Perkins Hall, on the northwest corner of Edith Street and Central Avenue. The building was eventually rented to the later public school system and served as the first public library building.

In 1892, a public school system was created, and a contract was let for the construction of four ward school buildings placed roughly equidistant in the city. The structures were completed in 1893, and in 1900, a middle and high school building, the Central School, was built at Lead Avenue and Third Street."[95]

**How did the idea of a University in Albuquerque come about? What citizen fought most for its proposal to the legislature?**

The idea began with Governor Donaciano Vigil shortly after the American Occupation and was originally supposed to be within a mile of Santa Fe. Bernard Rodey came to Albuquerque from Boston, became a lawyer here, and was elected to the legislature. He led the fight for the establishment of New Mexico Agricultural College, the School of Mines (Socorro), and the Territorial University at Albuquerque.

**After the first building at UNM was completed, what was the cost of tuition for a four-year program?**

Tuition was free but there was a $3.00 matriculation fee for the support of the library.

**What was the number of students in the graduating class of 1914 at the University of New Mexico?**

Eight graduates. A little over 100 students were enrolled at the time. In the fall of 2005, there were 26,280 students enrolled at the Main Campus of UNM, with another 6,635 students enrolled at the other four campuses of UNM: Gallup, Los Alamos, Valencia and Taos.

**What significant change occurred on campus when a former UNM President became infatuated with the pueblo style of architecture?**

The most significant early change occurred about 1906-08 when President Tight became infatuated with the Pueblo style of architecture. He had Hodgin Hall remodeled in the style and designed other new buildings in the motif. Regents of the University were not pleased and they dismissed Tight for this and other reasons. In 1910, the University had only a few buildings. The men's dormitory was named Kwataka (in Pueblo language, 'man eagle') and the women's dormitory was named Hokona ('virgin butterfly' in Pueblo language).[96]

Hodgin Hall in winter, UNM, 1920. Photographer Milner Studio. The Albuquerque Museum Photoarchives, PA1992.5.615.

**What is the state's most comprehensive institution of higher education?**

The University of New Mexico enters its second century of service, offering degrees ranging from the AA to the Ph.D. in 125 different fields. UNM offers 210 certificate and degree programs at its main and branch campuses. UNM's medicine and pharmacy programs consistently rank among the best nationwide. The clinical law program was ranked 8th nationally.[97]

UNM is nationally and internationally recognized for its programs in anthropology, biology, Latin American studies, and medicine. It also leads the way for the arts in Albuquerque by supporting four theaters for the performing arts and eight museums or galleries for artists and sculptors. There also are a museum of anthropology, a biology museum, a geology museum, and a meteorite museum.

**Who was it that introduced the idea of kindergarten to Albuquerque?**

Ada Philbrick. She introduced the idea of kindergarten, a German concept of preschool education, to Albuquerque when it was as novel as modern Montessori preschools. Miss Philbrick's kindergarten was a great success. Erna Fergusson, the author, was among her pupils.[98]

**How many branches of the Public Library can one find in Albuquerque?**

Besides the Main Library at 501 Copper Ave. NW, there are also fifteen branches located throughout the metro area, in addition to a Special Collections Library that houses research collections on genealogy and New Mexico history.

**What are the team/mascot names of the public high schools within Albuquerque city limits?**

ALBUQUERQUE PUBLIC HIGH SCHOOLS

| **School name** | **Mascot** |
|---|---|
| Albuquerque High School | Bulldogs |
| Cibola High School | Cougars |
| Del Norte High School | Knights |
| Eldorado High School | Eagles |
| Highland High School | Hornets |
| La Cueva High School | Bears |
| Manzano High School | Monarchs |
| Rio Grande High School | Ravens |
| Sandia High School | Matadors |
| Valley High School | Vikings |
| West Mesa High School | Mustangs |

**What was Albuquerque's first high school?**

Albuquerque High School, which was established in 1879.

**What is the Central New Mexico Community College?**

Formerly the Albuquerque Technical-Vocational Institute, CNM is a public community college that was created to provide vocational and technical education at the post-high school level. It was established in 1965 to provide adults with marketable skills and the related education needed to succeed in an occupation. More than 26,000 students currently attend classes at the four campuses (Main Campus, Montoya Campus, South Valley Campus, and Westside Campus) and at a Workforce Training Center in the Albuquerque area.[99]

**Who was the first President of UNM?**

Elias Stover, a city businessman, was elected by the Board of Regents in 1899.

**What is significant about the Old Main Library, now the Special Collections Branch Library?**

The 1890 brick school building on the property was the first Albuquerque Academy. It served as the city library from 1901 to 1924. The Old Main Library was built in 1925 on land donated to the city by Joshua and Sarah Raynolds. A prominent Santa Fe artist was hired to do interior decorating. The building is an example of Spanish-Pueblo Revival architecture. In addition to the major research collections in genealogy and New Mexico history, the library contains a museum of the history of books and printing, The Center for the Book.[100]

**1951** Before you read on, try to guess the intersection at the center of the photo and the names of the two neighborhoods visible in this aerial photo made by Bill Laskar in Albuquerque in 1951. Give up? The intersection is Menaul and Wyoming boulevards Northeast. The neighborhoods are the Hoffmantown (at right) and Inez (at left). The curved structure just to the left of center is the Hoffmantown shopping center. Visible in the upper right is the dirt landing strip that Harold Snell operated near his home on North Pennsylvania Street. Barely visible in the upper left is the Belair subdivision along Menaul and Carlisle boulevards Northeast.

Intersection of Menaul and Wyoming, 1951. Hoffmantown Shopping Center is visible to the left of center. Photograph provided by Neilmarie Salon in Hoffmantown Shopping Center.

Bison herd grazing on Sandia Pueblo land; Sandia Mountains in background.

Snow-capped Sandia Peak in Spring.

# References

[1] Dennis Domrzalski, "High Runners," *Accent Albuquerque* May 2006: 16-17.

[2] Marc Simmons, *Albuquerque* (Albuquerque: University of New Mexico Press, 1982) 18.

[3] Simmons 16.

[4] "Duke City Hits 100 For First Time Since 1999," *Albuquerque Journal* 1 July 2002: B-8, *NewsLibrary,* 6 July 2006 http://nl.newsbank.com/nl-search/we/Archives?p_action=print&p_docid=OF486323DB2A6....

[5] "Warmth Sets A Record in N.M.," *Albuquerque Journal* 17 Dec. 2003, *NewsLibrary,* 29 June 2006 http://nl.newsbank.com/nl-search/we/Archives.

[6] "The day it was so cold city life almost stopped," *The Albuquerque Tribune* 1 Feb. 1997: C-1, *NewsLibrary*, 7 July 2006 http://nl.newsbank.com/nl-search/we/Archives?p_action=print&p_docid=10955B4405BC5....

[7] Albuquerque Museum.

[8] "Forbes: The best cities to start a business—or a career," *MSN Money,* 19 May 2005, 10 July 2006 http://moneycentral.msn.com/content/invest/forbes/P118734.asp.

[9] "Albuquerque Rankings – Why Albuquerque?" *Economic Development – City of Albuquerque,* 7 June 2006, 7 June 2006 http://www.cabq.gov/econdev/whyabqrankings.html.

[10] Jack Kutz, *Mysteries & Miracles of New Mexico (*Corrales, NM: Rhombus Publishing Company, 1988) 176.

[11] "Trivia," *Albuquerque Tricentennial,* 19 July 2006 http://www.albuquerque300.org/index.aspx?temp=16&edit=0&pk=54&tk=373.

[12] Michael McDonald, *The Quiz of Enchantment* (Santa Fe: New Mexico Magazine, 1992) 40.

[13] Barbara Taylor, ed., "With the First Bite You Are a Chile Addict," *The Tribune* 21 Nov. 1966: B-1.

[14] Randi Hutter Epstein, (The Associated Press, London) "Chile Might Help Ulcer Sufferers," *Albuquerque Journal* 20 May 1995: A-4.

[15] "The Whittlesey House. 201 Highland Park Circle SE, 1903, Charles Whittlesey," *City of Albuquerque*, 7 June 2006 http://www.cabq.gov/planning/lucc/whittlesey.html.

[16] Frank Zoretich, "New Mexico ghost hunters sample the spooks," *The Albuquerque Tribune Online,* 12 Sept. 2006 http://www.sgha.net/AlbuquerqueTribune.html.

[17] McDonald 78.

[18] Marian Meyer, "It's One of Those Nutty Years," *Empire Magazine*, 15 Sept. 1974.

[19] Anthony Dellaflora, "A Day of Pride," *Albuquerque Journal* 22 Oct. 2000: A-1.

[20] "Maloof Family Biographies," *Kings,* 11 July 2006 http://www.nba.com/kings/news/Joe_and_Gavin_Maloof_Bio.html.

[21] "Las Mañanitas, 1800 Rio Grande Boulevard NW, Mid-19th Century, Architect Unknown," *City of Albuquerque*, 7 June 2006 http://www.cabq.gov/planning/lucc/lasmananitas.html.

[22] "History – Sports," *Albuquerque Tricentennial*, 26 July 2006 http://www.albuquerque300.org/index.aspx?pk=215&temp=2.

[23] Kelly Koepke, "Albuquerque The Interview: Alisa Valdes-Rodriguez," *Albuquerque The Magazine* July, 2006: 84-87.

[24] "About Us," *Bueno Foods,* 22 July 2006 http://www.buenofoods.com/aboutus.htm.

[25] "Bill Gates, Founder of Microsoft," *Vault Career Information*, 15 Aug. 2006 http://www.vault.com/nr/main_article_detail.jsp?article_id=19106&cat_id=0&ht_type=2.

[26] Stacey Reitz, "William Henry Gates III," *Virginia Tech Computer Science Department's National Science Foundation Education Infrastructure Project,* 29 Sept, 1996, 15 Aug. 2006 http://ei.cs.vt.edu/~history/Gates.html.

[27] Byron A. Johnson and Robert K. Dauner, eds., *Early Albuquerque* (Albuquerque: Albuquerque Journal, City of Albuquerque, Albuquerque Museum, 1981) 162.

[28] Johnson 194.

[29] Johnson 194.

[30] Johnson 195.

[31] "KiMo Theatre – History," *City of Albuquerque,* 22 June 2006, 22 June 2006 http://www.cabq.gov/kimo/history.html.

[32] David Steinberg, "Return to Glory," *Albuquerque Journal* 10 Sept. 2000: F-2.

[33] "History," *New Mexico Symphony Orchestra,* 22 June 2006 http://www.nmso.org/About/history.php.

[34] "Casa San Ysidro History," *City of Albuquerque,* 18 July 2006 http://www.cabq.gov/museum/history/casainfo.html.

[35] "Behind The Scenes. The Numbers Add Up!" *Albuquerque International Balloon Fiesta,* 27 June 2006 http://www.balloonfiesta.com/Education/History/numbers.php.

[36] Balloon Fiesta Final Statistics," *Albuquerque International Balloon Fiesta,* 27 June 2006 http://www.balloonfiesta.com/scripts/index/message_query.php?id=417.

[37] "Behind the Scenes. Hot Air Balloon Facts," *Albuquerque International Balloon Fiesta,* 27 June 2006 http://www.balloonfiesta.com/Education/History/facts.php.

[38] Simmons 39.

[39] Hatchet, *Historical Documents*, 3:379 as quoted in Marc Simmons, *Albuquerque* 81.

[40] Simmons 81-82.

[41] Lino Duarte Insua, *Historia de Albuquerque (*Badajoz, Spain: Tip. De Antonio Arqueros, 1929) as quoted in Marc Simmons, *Albuquerque* 92.

[42] Robert Wood, et al., "Albuquerque's Environmental Story. Educating For a Sustainable Community. Central Avenue as an Alpha Street. History of Central Avenue," *City of Albuquerque,* 2006, 17 Sept. 2006 http://www.cabq.gov/aes/s2p2hist.html.

[43] "History," *Manzano Day School,* 2006, 26 Sept. 2006 http://www.manzanodayschool.org/about.cfm?subpage=23908.

[44] Johnson 246-248.

[45] Johnson 149.

[46] Erna Fergusson, *Albuquerque* (Albuquerque: Merle Armitag Editions, 1947) 42.

[47] Johnson 148.

[48] Johnson 162-163.

[49] Ollie Reed Jr., "Marshall Drill'em," *The Albuquerque Tribune Online,* 24 Oct. 2006 http://web.abqtrib.com/archives/tourism01/020101_tales.shtml.

[50] "Former Ambassador Edward L. Romero; American Embassy, Madrid Spain," *Embasssy of the United States – Spain,* 2 Oct. 2002, 2 Aug. 2006 http://www.embusa.es/emba/amboeng.html.

[51] "Edward Romero, former U.S. ambassador to Spain, appointed to Bank of America board of directors," *Bank of America,* 26 June 2003, 2 Aug. 2006 http://newsroom.bankofamerica.com/index.php?s=press_releases&item=5553.

[52] "Dennis Chávez," *Library of Congress,* 12 Oct. 2006 http://www.loc.gov/rr/hispanic/congress/chavez.html.

[53] "Trivia," *Albuquerque Tricentennial,* 19 July 2006 http://www.albuquerque300.org/index.aspx?temp=168&edit=0&pk=54&tk=88.

[54] The Albuquerque Convention & Visitors Bureau, http://www.itsatrip.org.

[55] Albuquerque Museum.

[56] Johnson 74.

[57] Johnson 96-97.

[58] Johnson 97.

[59] "Blake's Lotaburger," *Wikipedia – the free encyclopedia,* 8 July 2006, 17 July 2006 http://en.wikipedia.org/wiki/Blake's_Lotaburger.

[60] "More Data. Demographics. Census Counts of New Mexico Municipalities, 1910-2003," *New Mexico Economic Development Department,* 4 Jan. 2007 http://ww1.edd.state.nm.us/index.php?/data/C31/.

[61] "Albuquerque Quick Facts," *City of Albuquerque,* 19 July 2006 http://www.cabq.gov/econdev/whyabqquickfacts.html.

[62] Albuquerque Museum.

[63] "The History," *Kelly's Brew Pub,* 2005, 19 Sept. 2006 http://www.kellysbrewpub.com/pages/history.html.

[64] Johnson 190.

[65] Johnson 204.

[66] "History – Sports," *Albuquerque Tricentennial,* 26 July 2006 http://www.albuquerque300.org/index.aspx?pk=215&temp=2.

[67] Dennis Latta, "It's Time to Bid Farewell," *Albuquerque Journal,* 23 Aug. 2000, 30 Aug. 2000 http://www.abqjournal.com/sports/106110sports08-23-00.htm.

[68] "Albuquerque Isotopes Baseball," *New Mexico Tourism Department,* 2005, 31 Dec. 2006 http://www.newmexico.org/place/loc/directory/page/DB-place/category/179/place/726.html.

[69] "Johnny Tapia," *Wikipedia – the free encyclopedia,14 Oct. 2006,* 26 Oct. 2006 http://en.wikipedia.org/wiki/Johnny_Tapia.

[70] "Danny Romero," *Wikipedia – the free encyclopedia,14 Oct. 2006,* 26 Oct. 2006 http://en.wikipedia.org/wiki/Danny_Romero.

[71] "History – Sports," *Albuquerque Tricentennial,* 26 July 2006 http://www.albuquerque300.org/index.aspx?pk=215&temp=2.

[72] "New Mexico Lobo Basketball," *Wikipedia – the free encyclopedia,* 23 Dec. 2006, 31 Dec. 2006 http://en.wikipedia.org/wiki/New_Mexico_Lobo_Basketball.

[73] "UNM Mourns passing of Bob King," *UNM Today,* 10 Dec. 2004, 29 Aug. 2006 http://www.unm.edu/~market/cgi-bin/archives/000434.html.

[74] "Kenny Thomas," *Wikipedia – the free encyclopedia,* 18 Aug. 2006, 29 Aug. 2006 http://en.wikipedia.org/wiki/Kenny_Thomas.

[75] Mike Hall, "Holm Starting to Merit Notice Nationally," *Albuquerque Journal Online Edition,* 8 Sept. 2006, 12 Sept. 2006 http://www.abqjournal.com/sports/490839sports09-08-06.htm.

[76] Richard Stevens, "Boxer knows she needs to market more than her record," *Scripps Howard News Service,* 13 Nov. 2005, 12 Sept. 2006 http://www.knoxstudio.com/shns/story.cfm?pk=BOX-HOLLYHOLM-11-13-05&cat=BW.

[77] Nasario Garcia with Richard McCord, *Albuquerque ¡Feliz Cumpleaños! Three Centuries to Remember* (Santa Fe, NM: Gran Vía Incorporated, 2005) 64.

[78] "Diego Sánchez," *Wikipedia – the free encyclopedia* 27 Oct. 2006, 28 Oct. 2006 http://en.wikipedia.org/wiki/Diego_S%C3%A1nchez.

[79] "Hall of Fame. L.F. 'Tow' Diehm," *New Mexico Athletic Trainers Association, Inc.,* 31 Oct. 2006 http://nmathletictrainers.org/tow.html.

[80] "On This Day/17 August/1978: U.S. balloonists' record Atlantic crossing," *BBC News,* 31 Dec. 2006 http://news.bbc.co.uk/onthisday/low/dates/stories/august/17/newsid_2534000/2534525.stm.

[81] Johnson 205.

[82] Don E. Alberts, *Balloons to Bombers: Aviation in Albuquerque, 1882-1945* (Albuquerque: The Albuquerque Museum, 1987) 37.

[83] "Old Airport Terminal. 2920 Yale SE, 1939, Ernest Blumenthal," *City of Albuquerque,* 13 Sept. 2006 http://www.cabq.gov/planning/lucc/airport.html.

[84] McDonald 2.

[85] McDonald 76.

[86] Johnson 32.

[87] Simmons 13.

[88] "History – Place Names," *Albuquerque Tricentennial,* 26 July 2006 http://www.albuquerque300.org/index.aspx?pk=214&temp=2.

[89] "History – Place Names."

[90] "History – Land Grants," *Albuquerque Tricentennial,* 26 July 2006 http://www.albuquerque300.org/index.aspx?pk=208&temp=2.

[91] "History – Land Grants."

[92] "Roosevelt Park. Coal/Spruce/Sycamore SE, 1933, C. Edmund 'Bud' Hollied," *City of Albuquerque,* 13 Sept. 2006 http://www.cabq.gov/planning/lucc/roosvelt.html.

[93] "Inventory of the Erna Fergusson Papers, 1846-1964/Collection number: MSS 45 BC/Biography," *The University of New Mexico, General Library. Center for Southwest Research,* May 2001, 8 Jan. 2007 http://elibrary.unm.edu/oanm/NmU/nmu1%23mss45bc/nmu1%23mss45bc_m1.html.

[94] Johnson 127.

[95] Johnson 214-215.

[96] Johnson 215, 226-227.

[97] "About UNM," *UNM,* 5 Aug. 2005, 19 June 2006 http://www.unm.edu/about.html.

[98] Johnson 215.

[99] "CNM History," *CNM,* 16 June 2006, 17 June 2006 http://www.tvi.edu/depts/pio/media/History.php.

[100] "Old Main Library. 423 Central NE, 1925, Arthur Rossiter," *City of Albuquerque,* 13 Sept. 2006 http://www.cabq.gov/planning/lucc/omainlibrary.html.

# Works Cited


"About UNM." UNM. 5 Aug. 2005. 19 June 2006. http://www.unm.edu/about.html.

"About Us." Bueno Foods. 22 July 2006. http://www.buenofoods.com/aboutus.htm.

Alberts, Don E., Balloons to Bombers: Aviation in Albuquerque, 1882-1945. Albuquerque: The Albuquerque Museum, 1987.

"Albuquerque Isotopes Baseball." New Mexico Tourism Department. 2005. 31 Dec. 2006. http://www.newmexico.org/place/loc/directory/page/DB-place/category/179/place/726.html.

"Albuquerque Quick Facts." City of Albuquerque. 19 July 2006. http://www.cabq.gov/econdev/whyabqquickfacts.html.

"Albuquerque Rankings – Why Albuquerque?" Economic Development – City of Albuquerque. 7 June 2006. 7 June 2006. http://www.cabq.gov/econdev/whyabqrankings.html.

"Behind the Scenes. Hot Air Balloon Facts." Albuquerque International Balloon Fiesta. 27 June 2006. http://www.balloonfiesta.com/Education/History/facts.php.

"Behind The Scenes. The Numbers Add Up!" Albuquerque International Balloon Fiesta. 27 June 2006. http://www.balloonfiesta.com/Education/History/numbers.php.

"Bill Gates, Founder of Microsoft." Vault Career Information. 15 Aug. 2006. http://www.vault.com/nr/main_article_detail.jsp?article_id=19106&cat_id=0&ht_type=2.

"Blake's Lotaburger." Wikipedia – the free encyclopedia. 8 July 2006. 17 July 2006. http://en.wikipedia.org/wiki/Blake's_Lotaburger.

"Casa San Ysidro History." City of Albuquerque. 18 July 2006. http://www.cabq.gov/museum/history/casainfo.html.

"CNM History." CNM. 16 June 2006. 17 June 2006. http://www.tvi.edu/depts/pio/media/History.php.

"Danny Romero." Wikipedia – the free encyclopedia. 14 Oct. 2006. 26 Oct. 2006. http://en.wikipedia.org/wiki/Danny_Romero.

Dellaflora, Anthony. "A Day of Pride." Albuquerque Journal 22 Oct. 2000: A-1.

"Dennis Chávez." Library of Congress. 12 Oct. 2006. http://www.loc.gov/rr/hispanic/congress/chavez.html.

"Diego Sánchez." Wikipedia – the free encyclopedia. 27 Oct. 2006. 28 Oct. 2006. http://en.wikipedia.org/wiki/Diego_S%C3%A1nchez.

Domrzalski, Dennis. "High Runners." Accent Albuquerque May, 2006: 16-17.

"Duke City Hits 100 For First Time Since 1999," Albuquerque Journal 1 July 2002: B-8. NewsLibrary. 6 July 2006.

http://nl.newsbank.com/nl-search/we/Archives?p_action=print&p_docid=OF486323DB2A6....

"Edward Romero, former U.S. ambassador to Spain, appointed to Bank of America board of directors," 26 June 2003. Bank of America. 2 Aug. 2006. http://newsroom.bankofamerica.com/index.php?s=press_release&item=5553.

Fergusson, Erna. Albuquerque. Albuquerque: Merle Armitag Editions, 1947.

"Forbes: The best cities to start a business—or a career." MSN Money. 19 May 2005. 10 July 2006. http://moneycentral.msn.com/content/invest/forbes/P118734.asp.

"Former Ambassador Edward L. Romero; American Embassy, Madrid Spain." Embasssy of the United States – Spain. 2 Oct. 2002. 2 Aug. 2006. http://www.embusa.es/emba/amboeng.html.

Garcez, Antonio R. Adobe Angels (The Ghosts of Albuquerque). Santa Fe, NM: Red Rabbit Press, 1994.

Garcia, Nasario with McCord, Richard. Albuquerque ¡Feliz Cumpleaños! Three Centuries to Remember. Santa Fe, NM: Gran Vía Incorporated, 2005.

"Hall of Fame. L.F. 'Tow' Diehm.'" New Mexico Athletic Trainers Association, Inc. 31 Oct. 2006. http://nmathletictrainers.org/tow.html.

Hall, Mike, "Holm Starting to Merit Notice Nationally." Albuquerque Journal Online Edition. 8 Sept. 2006. 12 Sept. 2006. http://www.abqjournal.com/sports/490839sports09-08-06.htm.

Hatchet, Historical Documents, 3:379 as quoted in Simmons, Marc, Albuquerque: 81.

"History – Land Grants." Albuquerque Tricentennial. 26 July 2006. http://www.albuquerque300.org/index.aspx?pk=208&temp=2.

"History." Manzano Day School. 2006. 20 Sept. 2006. http://www.manzanodayschool.org/about.cfm?subpage=23908.

"History." New Mexico Symphony Orchestra. 22 June 2006. http://www.nmso.org/About/history.php.

"History – Place Names." Albuquerque Tricentennial. 26 July 2006. http://www.albuquerque300.org/index.aspx?pk=214&temp=2.

"History – Sports." Albuquerque Tricentennial. 26 July 2006. http://www.albuquerque300.org/index.aspx?pk=215&temp=2.

Hutter Epstein, Randi. (The Associated Press, London.) "Chile Might Help Ulcer Sufferers." Albuquerque Journal 20 May 1995: A-4.

Insua, Lino Duarte. Historia de Albuquerque. Badajoz, Spain: Tip. De Antonio Arqueros: 1929, as quoted in Simmons, Marc, Albuquerque: 92.

"Inventory of the Erna Fergusson Papers, 1846-1964/Collection number: MSS 45 BC/Biography." The University of New Mexico, General Library. Center for Southwest Research. May 2001. 8 Jan. 2007 http://elibrary.unm.edu/oanm/NmU/nmu1%23mss45bc/nmu1%23mss45bc_m4.html.

"Johnny Tapia." Wikipedia – the free encyclopedia. 14 Oct. 2006. 26 Oct. 2006. http://en.wikipedia.org/wiki/Johnny_Tapia.

Johnson, Byron A. and Dauner, Robert K., eds., Early Albuquerque. Albuquerque: Albuquerque Journal, City of Albuquerque, Albuquerque Museum, 1981.

"Kenny Thomas." Wikipedia – the free encyclopedia. 18 Aug. 2006. 29 Aug. 2006. http://en.wikipedia.org/wiki/Kenny_Thomas.

"KiMo Theatre – History." City of Albuquerque. 22 June 2006. 22 June 2006. http://www.cabq.gov/kimo/history.html.

Koepke, Kelly. "Albuquerque The Interview: Alisa Valdes-Rodriguez." Albuquerque The Magazine July, 2006: 84-87.

Kutz, Jack. Mysteries & Miracles of New Mexico. Corrales, NM: Rhombus Publishing Company, 1988.

"Las Mañanitas. 1800 Rio Grande Boulevard NW, Mid-19th Century, Architect Unknown." City of Albuquerque. 7 June 2006. http://www.cabq.gov/planning/lucc/lasmananitas.html.

Latta, Dennis, "It's Time to Bid Farewell." Albuquerque Journal 23 Aug. 2000. 30 Aug. 2000. http://www.abqjournal.com/sports/106110sports08-23-00.htm.

"Maloof Family Biographies." Kings. 11 July 2006. http://www.nba.com/kings/news/Joe_and_Gavin_Maloof_Bio.html.

McDonald, Michael. The Quiz of Enchantment. Santa Fe: New Mexico Magazine, 1992.

Meyer, Marian. "It's One of Those Nutty Years." Empire Magazine 15 Sept. 1974.

"More Data. Demographics. Census Counts of New Mexico Municipalities, 1910-2003." New Mexico Economic Development Department. 4 Jan. 2007. http://ww1.edd.state.nm.us/index.php?/data/C31/.

"New Mexico Lobo Basketball." Wikipedia – the free encyclopedia. 23 Dec. 2006. 31 Dec. 2006. http://en.wikipedia.org/wiki/New_Mexico_Lobo_Basketball.

"Old Airport Terminal. 2920 Yale SE, 1939, Ernest Blumenthal." City of Albuquerque. 13 Sept. 2006. http://www.cabq.gov/planning/lucc/airport.html.

"Old Main Library. 423 Central NE, 1925, Arthur Rossiter." City of Albuquerque. 13 Sept. 2006. http://www.cabq.gov/planning/lucc/omainlibrary.html.

"On This Day/17 August/1978: U.S. balloonists' record Atlantic crossing." BBC News. 31 Dec. 2006. http://news.bbc.co.uk/onthisday/low/dates/stories/august/17/newsid_2534000/2534525.stm.

Reed, Ollie Jr. "Marshall Drill-em." The Albuquerque Tribune Online. 24 Oct. 2006. http://web.abqtrib.com/archives/tourism01/020101_tales.shtml.

Reitz, Stacey. "William Henry Gates III." Virginia Tech Computer Science Department's National Science Foundation Education Infrastructure Project. 29 Sept. 1996. 15 Aug. 2006. http://ei.cs.vt.edu/~history/Gates.html.

"Roosevelt Park. Coal/Spruce/Sycamore SE, 1933, C. Edmund 'Bud' Hollied." City of Albuquerque. 13 Sept. 2006. http://www.cabq.gov/planning/lucc/roosvelt.html.

Sandoval, Richard C. One of Our Fifty is Missing (A Continuing Saga). Santa Fe: New Mexico Publications Group, 1986.

Simmons, Marc. Albuquerque. Albuquerque: University of New Mexico Press, 1982.

Steinberg, David. "Return to Glory," Albuquerque Journal 10 Sept. 2000: F-2.

Stevens, Richard, "Boxer knows she needs to market more than her record." Scripps Howard News Service. 13 Nov. 2005. 12 Sept. 2006. http://www.knoxstudio.com/shns/story.cfm?pk=BOX-HOLLYHOLM-11-13-05&cat=BW.

Taylor, Barbara, ed. "With the First Bite You Are a Chile Addict," The Tribune 21 Nov. 1966: B-1.

"The day it was so cold city life almost stopped," The Albuquerque Tribune 1 Feb. 1997: C-1. NewsLibrary. 7 July

2006. http://nl.newsbank.com/nl-search/we/Archives?p_action=print&p_docid=10955B4405BC5....

"The History." Kelly's Brew Pub. 2005. 19 Sept. 2006 http://www.kellysbrewpub.com/pages/history.html.

"The Whittlesey House. 201 Highland Park Circle SE, 1903, Charles Whittlesey." City of Albuquerque. 7 June 2006. http://www.cabq.gov/planning/lucc/whittlesey.html.

"Trivia." Albuquerque Tricentennial. 19 July 2006. http://www.albuquerque300.org/index.aspx?temp=168&edit=0&pk=54&tk=88.

"Trivia." Albuquerque Tricentennial. 19 July 2006. http://www.albuquerque300.org/index.aspx?temp=16&edit=0&pk=54&tk=373.

"UNM Mourns passing of Bob King." UNM Today. 10 Dec. 2004. 29 Aug. 2006. http://www.unm.edu/ ~market/cgi-bin/archives/000434.html.

"Warmth Sets A Record in N.M.," Albuquerque Journal, 17 Dec. 2003. NewsLibrary. 29 June 2006. http://nl.newsbank.com/nl-search/we/Archives.

Wood, Robert et al., "Albuquerque's Environmental Story. Educating For a Sustainable Community. Central Avenue as an Alpha Street. History of Central Avenue." City of Albuquerque. 2006. 17 Sept. 2006. http://www.cabq.gov/aes/s2p2hist.html.

Zoretich, Frank. "New Mexico ghost hunters sample the spooks." The Albuquerque Tribune Online. 12 Sept. 2006. http://www.sgha.net/AlbuquerqueTribune.html.

"2005 Balloon Fiesta Final Statistics." Albuquerque International Balloon Fiesta. 27 June 2006. http://www.balloonfiesta.com/scripts/index/message_query.php?id=417.